Are We on the Same Te

ARE WE ON THE SAME TEAM HERE?

*Essential communication skills
to make groups work*

CAROLINE BREM

ALLEN & UNWIN

First published in 1995
Allen & Unwin Pty Ltd
9 Atchison Street, St Leonards, NSW 2065 Australia

National Library of Australia
Cataloguing-in-Publication entry:

Brem, Caroline.
    Are we on the same team here?

    Includes index.
    ISBN 1 86373 805 3.

    1. Work groups. 2. Communication in organizations. I. Title.

658.4036

Set in 11.5/13.5 pt Bembo by DOCUPRO, Sydney
Printed by SRM Production Services Sdn Bhd, Malaysia

10 9 8 7 6 5 4 3 2

CONTENTS

Preface   vii

Introduction   ix

1   Communication skills   1

2   Creation   11

3   Conflict   30

4   Cohesion   51

5   Construction   73

6   Crumbling   86

Checklist   95

Index   97

To Elyssebeth Leigh, who gave me a job when I didn't know I wanted one, and Janet Miller, who didn't give me one when I thought I did.

If I CANNOT be free,
To do such work as pleases me,
Near woodland pools and under trees,
You'll get no work at all; for I
Would rather live this life and die
A beggar or a thief, than be
A working slave with no days free.

WH Davies, 'No Master'

PREFACE

THIS BOOK CAME about because I couldn't find a text that was suitable for the work-team communications courses I was teaching. Experiential learning—learning by doing—is all very well when students are given a good theoretical basis. In most of our courses there just didn't seem to be enough time to get through all the theory and still allow the students to work as a group. What was needed, I felt, was a book which would deliver the theory in an easy-to-read format. Class time could then be used for practice and discussion, and the book would become a reference for later revision.

Learning is not something which happens only in the classroom; groups or teams are not only found at work. We need to be aware of all the overlaps: that something learned in one situation can be used in another. It may need some adaptation, some small refinement, but with practice we learn to take skills from one area of our lives to another. In the end this can only improve our ability to cope with the complex world we live in.

Nothing comes from nothing and it's hard to do things on your own so although I didn't actually work with a group of writers on this book, I do owe a great debt of gratitude to a number of people. The English/Communications teachers at Granville TAFE College were always happy to share their time and resources. Special thanks to Janet Murray and Denise Sheridan who read parts of the manuscript and commented constructively; Margaret Lackenby who helped me develop some of the material and who listened patiently to my theorising; Phua Seng Min who gave me groups of students on whom to use my material. And, of course, thanks to all the students who have worked so hard and shown me the strengths as well as the weaknesses of my theories. Thanks also to Mark Treddinick, my publisher, and Jo Jarrah, production editor, from Allen & Unwin.

To my own group—my family—I am grateful for the time and space they gave me; for 'allowing' me a room of my own and for 'allowing' me not to do more than my fair share of the chores.

I'm sure there are others who may feel that they should have been singled out for thanks and I offer them my apologies for any oversight.

INTRODUCTION

WORKING IN A team is something you've prob-
ably done more often than you realise. After all, families are teams,
sport is often played by teams, any committee is a team, in fact any
group of people who have a common goal makes up a team. This
means that you are very likely to have a lot of the skills which are
necessary for team work, even if you haven't actually thought them
through.

As we meet new situations in our lives, we can usually draw on
previous experiences to help us through. Sometimes we need to
modify our experiences a little to make them fit into the present
situation, and we usually could use some help to see how to make
those changes.

It would be extremely difficult for me to give you a solution to
every problem which could possibly arise in a group: there are far
too many variables. I do believe, though, that by examining the
situation and then reading something about the feelings, the actions,
the reactions and the interactions which are operating, we quite often
find solutions unexpectedly. We need to have faith in our ability to
tap into our own subconscious minds; to take advantage of our
accumulated experiences and use them in new combinations.

Your experiences may not come from the same kind of group as that of which you now find yourself a part, but that isn't really important: most of the experiences will have some relationship to what happens in the new kind of group. After all, the way Aunt Hattie behaves at family gatherings is likely to be similar to the way Mr McGraw from Accounts carries on at the sales meetings, and you'll probably find that you can deal with Mr McGraw the same way that Granny handles Aunt Hattie.

If you aren't already part of a work team, chances are you soon will be. Industry has been making the change to team work for quite some time now and it is a decided improvement on the way Henry Ford designed the production line. Instead of putting the same screw in the same hole in the same component part of a larger process day after day, we will now become part of a small group involved in a complete project. This has ramifications which we need to think about. For those of us who have been working on production lines, it will mean a major rethink of our work practices. For those of us who have been responsible for entire projects on our own, it will mean adjustment to a group. Either way, group communication processes will have to be learnt. We have to realise that small groups of up to, say, eight members don't operate in the same way as large groups of, say, ten members upwards or very small groups of four or fewer. Once we put people into groups of five to eight, all sorts of interesting things start to happen. There may be personality clashes, there will be rivalry, there will be a certain amount of jostling for position.

This book will look at all these aspects of group functioning. We will look at some of the groups we may be part of in other areas of our lives besides work. You are probably part of a family group of some kind. It may be a nuclear family, an extended faimily, a share house or an alternate lifestyle commune. A committee you belong to, either at work or in your leisure time, is a group. You could be a member of a study group or you may be thinking of starting an interest group—anything from abacus collecting to Zoroastrian philosophy. Even when organisations grow quite big, there is usually a committee of some kind which takes responsibility for the running of the organisation.

It should be noted that small groups may not be the most cost-efficient way of finding solutions to problems. The main advantages of using the group method are that there will be more creativity and risk-taking in the search for solutions and far greater acceptance of the solution agreed on. When this happens there will also be higher productivity.

By using case studies to highlight each topic, this book can be used as a reference to solve immediate problems as well as being a sequential presentation of group communication and functioning.

I want the information to be accessible to people who suddenly find their work practices changing. Whether you have reached that magic age of 40 plus and feel that you still have quite a few good years of work ahead, or you are just starting your first job and feel that you are unsure of what will be expected of you, or you're anywhere in between and would like a little help to keep you up to date, this book will prove useful.

There are two ingredients in the interactions which take place in groups—content and process. Content is the subject matter or task the group is working on. This is where everyone's energy will be directed. Process is all that activity which is going on between group members, and how they feel about themselves and each other.

This book will deal with process, which is important, but because it is less obvious is usually overlooked. It is also the less understood ingredient of group interaction.

Broadly speaking there are two skills areas we will need to look at.

INTERPERSONAL COMMUNICATION SKILLS

These are the skills we need if we are to get other people to understand us and understand the information we are trying to pass on. We also need them to help us understand other people. In groups this is critical, because the group can only function well when members understand each other: not just on the language level, but also on an emotional level. Throughout this book, we will be learning about stress management, conflict resolution, listening, speaking, questioning and so on.

GROUP PROCESS SKILLS

These are needed when a group of people gets together and forms a team. Because of the roles people play, power struggles, and group 'rules', group members will need skills like assertiveness, tolerance and trust.

Groups go through various stages as they develop. We can think of the first stage as **creation**, sometimes an easy process, sometimes difficult, occasionally very fast and at other times a slow unfolding. The group can come together spontaneously or it could be brought together by some outside influence. In the case of work teams it is usually management which decides on the members of a group. Committees are either elected or selected by members of the larger group, and friendship groups form spontaneously.

Next comes **conflict** or sorting it all out and we all know the problems that can bring. Regardless of who chose the team members in the first place, there will be leadership struggles. There will be a time of getting to know one another; learning how to behave in this particular group.

The third stage is **cohesion** or getting it all together: a time when things begin to settle down, become serious—but not too serious—and the team spirit builds. Members will have learnt something about one another, but may still be a little unsure of what will happen next.

Stage four is **construction** or getting the job done: the group functions at a high level of commitment with individual members having enough freedom to perform tasks independently. By this time there is a fairly high level of trust and, because the group is united, decision making will be a reasonably easy process, although there can still be some heated discussions before agreement is reached.

The last stage is **crumbling** or falling apart: like all organisms, groups eventually reach an end point. In families this happens when the children grow up and leave and the unit begins to disintegrate. In groups this happens when the set task or tasks have been completed. Committees are usually dissolved after a set period and then reformed, often with some members remaining, some leaving and new ones coming in. This can change the dynamics of the final phase quite considerably. How we cope depends on how we have functioned in the past and how well we have prepared ourselves for this eventuality. Some of us find it quite easy to leave people and places and move on to new experiences; others, frightened of the unknown, cling to familiar things.

Whatever headings we use for the various stages of development, it is important to realise that some groups may spend more time at one or other of these stages than seems right. When this happens the group may disintegrate, lose its way and cease to exist, or it may muddle on. If it muddles on with the task in hand, but the process stops growing, members of the team will feel unhappy, frustrated, angry or disheartened. They may decide to leave the group, or they may just slow down and cause frustration to other members. Usually everyone will feel unhappy with the way the group is going and it will, in the end, fold.

Each stage in the life of a group is dealt with in a chapter of this book. There's also a preliminary chapter which discusses the vital issue of communication. The chapters are not of equal length. There is far more to learn in the first two stages, a little less in the third, less again in the fourth and, well, the fifth is like the end of anything: we don't like to dwell too much on death. Because of the structure I have used, I feel that the best way to use the book is by skimming through it first and then using the index to find the information you need when you have a specific problem. You may find that the problem you have is discussed in what seems to be the wrong part of the book. It's important to remember that you are dealing with human beings, and very little ever goes exactly according to someone else's plan. You may have a member who joins the group during an intermediate stage, but still has to go through some of the emotions and adjustments which other members made back in stage one. Then again, a valued member may leave before the group gets to stage five. The rest of the group may then, on a limited scale, go through the processes we'll discuss in chapter 6.

During the first stage—creation—we will need to learn about rejection and acceptance, about inclusion, belonging, being polite and cautious. At first it will seem like chaos. People will be testing one another while also being very polite, and yet it will still be everyone for themselves. And, as in other areas of life, we must realise that some groups never make it past this stage.

The second stage—conflict—is the time when members are concerned about power, control, status and authority so it isn't hard to see that we will need to know how to deal with conflict, power struggles and criticism. People are formal with each other, they are asking questions—why are we here?—they want to be included, but they are also trying to exert influence and see who else has influence. They want to be included, but are wary of how participating will affect them. Groups sometimes get stuck in this stage, too. When they do, they will still get the task done, but they won't be happy. Members will be constantly trying to assert themselves, without allowing others to do so.

In the third phase—cohesion—members begin to think of the group as a unit and there is more open-mindedness and affection between group members. This is when the real work begins to be done: when the group changes its focus from the process to the product. Features of this stage may include bids for power, building of trust, coalition and the growth of a team spirit. Groups don't often get stuck at this stage. By this time the group is beginning to develop some maturity and growth is a natural process. When groups break up during this stage it is usually due to outside influences or catastrophic and unforeseen events.

By the time the group reaches the fourth stage—construction—when members are able to agree to disagree and still give one another necessary support, they will all be more skillful at the roles they play in the group and there will be a feeling of interdependency. Again, this isn't a stage when things go badly wrong. By this stage the group is usually functioning well, getting things done, and is a cohesive whole.

Once we understand the stages and what happens in each one, we can figure out quite easily how to adapt our behaviour to fit in. This is useful when we join a group which is already operating. If we can see that the group has emerged from the conflict stage we can act in a non-confrontational way and so avoid being rejected. Anyone who doesn't behave in the way expected by other members will be thought of as a deviate. (We will discuss in chapter 5 how groups deal with deviates.)

Depending on the length of time the group has been together, the closeness members have achieved and the success they've met with, the final winding-up will be more or less painful for the individuals involved. In order to get through this stage—crumbling—

without too much trauma, we need to learn to deal with the emotions which will surface during this time. The group also needs a good social–emotional leader—a people person—who can deal with all these emotions.

There are other things which can go wrong with the process, but we will look at them more closely as we go through the various stages in detail.

One other situation which occasionally arises is that the group reaches a fairly advanced stage and then has one or two new members join it. In some cases a slight regression may take place. This could happen because the new members have not worked in teams before and need an induction period. It could also happen because the new members have been chosen by management and there may, at first, be some animosity between old and new members. If the group has built up any trust before the new arrivals join the team, it will take time for them to be admitted to this same level of trust. It's possible, by listening to the discussion in a meeting, to tell which stage a group has reached. This is a useful exercise when the task work appears to have slowed down for no apparent reason.

We need to remember that all groups experience these feelings, and this is the reason there is growth from one stage to the next. For the group to maintain a balance between interpersonal relationships and the task at hand, it must not get too caught up with feelings, especially negative ones.

It is not only up to the leader to ensure that things run smoothly. Every member of the team needs to make an effort to learn more about how groups function so that they can become more effective participants. After all, group membership is not a spectator sport: all members have to pull their weight.

1

COMMUNICATION SKILLS

WE ALL WANT to be good communicators, and yet we can all think of times when events went wrong because someone didn't understand us, or because we didn't understand them. Often we need a little help, a reminder that we are human and can easily lose our way in the communication maze.

This chapter is about the basics, about the ways that we can transfer information from one person to another.

VERBAL COMMUNICATION

The most obvious, the one we always think of first, is speech or verbal communication. All the others are forms of non-verbal communication: writing, sign languages of one sort or another, body language and even such things as the way we dress.

Speaking to one another is not always as simple as it sounds. All kinds of things can happen to cause communication breakdown. Let's look at the process and what it's made up of before we look at ways in which problems could arise.

For any communication to take place we need a sender, a receiver and a message.

There could be interference in the form of noise, distance, language mismatch or prejudice, to name just a few.

In order to overcome this interference, or to get around it, we would need to get some feedback. When you are the sender of the message you can build in requests for feedback by asking questions to make sure the receiver has understood what you have been saying. If you are the receiver make sure you signal your understanding of the message by such actions as a nod of the head, an interested look on your face or by restating the information being given.

Feedback and understanding are very much influenced by the background of the speaker. All the past experiences we've had affect not only the way we receive a message, but also the way we send one. And the most important experience we have of groups and how they work is the way the family we grew up in functioned. These early family experiences are the biggest factor in how we will function in adult life.

This doesn't mean we can't change; it means that we will only begin to change when we become conscious of our behaviour. After all, we have to see and realise that something is wrong, or unacceptable, before we will want to change it.

After families, the next most influential groups in most of our lives are friendship groups. This is especially true in adolescence when we are trying to break away from the family group and show our independence. The experiences we have in these groups—the family and the friendship group—will have a very strong influence on the way we behave in any other group we become part of. So, it is not only a language barrier that can arise but also an experiences barrier—and the block will be just as severe.

Feedback

If you are not sure that you have understood a message, then you must give feedback either by restating the message in your own words or by asking for more information. This will give the sender the chance to correct you if there is any misunderstanding, before anything else is said. You may know from experience that when a piece of information is misunderstood or misinterpreted early in a transaction, things will keep getting worse, and not until the first misunderstanding is cleared up will the situation improve. Like a snowball, a small mistake at the beginning can lead to ever bigger mistakes.

When a difference of language background is the cause of the interference it is even more important to get feedback and make sure that each person understands the message. There are, of course, occasions when verbal communication doesn't allow for feedback: radio (except for talk-back), television and movies. Next time you discuss a movie or a television show with a friend, think about the differences in your interpretations. This happens because we all bring our own ideas and past experiences into the way we understand new information.

Listening

You have to hear things in order to be able to listen to them, but just because you hear something doesn't mean that you are listening. Listening takes concentration. You have to pay attention, be interested and engage your mind in the process.

Too often we have fixed ideas which get in the way of the message someone is trying to send us. We hear a word we don't like—it could be anything: racism, AIDS, broccoli—and we immediately stop paying attention and start thinking of our own views on the subject. Or we think we know what the speaker is about to say because the particular subject is something we have some experience in. So we stop listening and start thinking about what we will say. It is impossible to give the speaker your full attention while you are trying to plan your next speech.

Of course, there are all sorts of other barriers to listening. There may be outside interference—other people talking; a radio playing loudly; traffic noise; machinery and movement in the background. You can probably think of at least one or two others. It takes practice, but you can learn to ignore all these and pay careful attention to the speaker.

Good listening starts with concentrating, goes on with involvement and needs lots of feedback. Don't stop listening because the subject matter seems difficult or boring. If it's difficult, try asking the speaker to clarify any points you have trouble with.

Harry thinks everyone can read his mind. He often starts a meeting

3

with this kind of information: 'Well, I spoke to them the other day and they said they would get all that stuff done for us by next week. I said that would be OK so we'll have to wait for them before we can go on.'

The rest of the group sits round the table looking puzzled but Harry doesn't notice. Because he's the chairman of the committee nobody says anything. They know that he will eventually say something which will clear this up. But it usually takes a while for this to happen.

It would be much simpler for someone to stop him and ask him to explain who 'they' are and what the 'stuff' is. This will probably save time later in the meeting: he is, after all, talking about something he was asked to arrange. Being the chairman, Harry was probably responsible for doing or arranging more than one thing before this meeting.

Eventually the committee got a new member who had no idea what Harry was talking about when he went on like this, and she asked for feedback. When she had done this three or four times, Harry began to be more aware of what he was doing. It still took a while for him to speak more accurately, but until the new member joined the group, he had not even realised what he was doing.

By listening carefully you will learn something new and next time someone speaks about the subject you will have some knowledge of it. We never learn anything new while we are speaking!

Before you start to argue, make sure that the speaker's point of view really is different to your own. She might just have a different way of saying the same thing. Listen all the way through the other person's speech before making any judgement.

Anneliese:	Mr Brown said that we should pay $200 for using that park for a picnic. This is because . . .
Michael:	How can we be expected to pay all that money when we aren't charging anyone?
Anneliese:	This is because he wasn't aware that we are not charging anyone.
Michael:	Well, why didn't you tell him?
Anneliese:	I then told him that the picnic was to give a special treat to the old people from our community and then he said that in this case we will not have to pay anything.

4

When English is not your first language you often try people's patience by sounding long-winded. Partly this happens when people are still thinking in their first language and have to translate everything they want to say, sentence by sentence or even word by word. Some people have irritating speech habits or strange accents.

Celia: There's a sort of parking problem, you know, in the local shopping centre sort of thing. The cars sort of park wherever there's a sort of space, like, you know, just anywhere. Even sort of on, you know, like the footpath and all.

Others have interesting material but speak in monotonous voices. All these make listening difficult, but if we hope to communicate effectively then we have to learn to ignore the distractions and irritations and concentrate on the information that is being presented.

Speaking

This concerns not only what we say but also the way that we say it. How you feel affects the way you sound. When you feel happy with yourself you'll find that you speak in an assertive way, taking other people's feelings and needs into consideration.

A good speaker is one who remembers these three points:

- choose the right words;
- speak clearly;
- make sure you are understood.

Choosing the right words is not always as simple as it sounds. You need to think about the person or people you are speaking to. Will they understand the words you are using? People for whom English is not the first language may have trouble with some words they haven't yet learned. They may not yet have the vocabulary necessary to understand all the activities related to their workplace. They may not understand slang or jargon. Don't confuse vocabulary with experience. Just because the person you are speaking to doesn't know the word 'locomotive', doesn't mean that he hasn't ever seen a locomotive before.

When you think the person you are speaking to has not understood what you have said, there are several things you can do. First, you can say the same thing, using simpler words. You can speak a little more slowly, but not too slowly. You could ask a question to find out what it is they have not understood. Or you could ask them to explain what they think you meant. These things should, however, be done with tact. It would be very easy to make the other person feel stupid if you said something like 'What exactly is it that you don't understand?' Rather, try more specific questions like, 'Have you been shown where Jane's office is?' said in a pleasant, friendly way. This will give the other person the opportunity to tell you what it is they do or do not know or understand.

When the other person is having trouble with their English it would help a lot if, as well as using simpler words, you make your sentences shorter. Instead of saying, 'When you finish mopping down the floor, and before you go into the office, please put all the chairs back where they belong', try this: 'First mop the floor. Then put all the chairs at the benches. Then go to the office'. It may sound a little stiff and formal but it is much clearer and easier to understand.

There is one rule you really should remember when speaking to someone who speaks a different language: shouting won't help them to understand. They aren't deaf, they just haven't learnt enough English words yet.

All this is tied up with speaking clearly—not just using the right words to make your meaning clear, but also making sure that the words sound correct when you say them. To speak clearly we need to feel confident—confident in ourselves and confident that we believe in what we have to say. Then it comes down to the mechanics of speech. Keep your head up, breathe deeply and then project your voice. We all hate listening to mumbling. You also have to remember not to put your hand across your mouth as you speak. Not only will people have trouble hearing what you are saying, they may also feel that they can't trust what you are saying.

Our third point for being a good speaker was to make sure you are understood. Apart from the advice we have already discussed, there are one or two other things which help. One of these is to ensure that the tone of voice we use matches the words we are speaking. Don't glare at anyone unless you are really angry, and never ever smile to 'soften' bad news, especially when you're talking to someone from a non-English-speaking background—they will be relying heavily on non-verbal clues. Not only does this distort your message, it lets the other person think you are harsh and unfeeling.

Another way to be easily understood is to use gestures and body language effectively. Use your hands to indicate things like size, shape and direction whenever possible. Make eye contact with the person you are speaking to. If there is more than one person, try to make eye contact with everyone at least once while you are speaking. This lets the listeners know that you are looking for feedback and lets you know that they are still listening and understanding. It's amazing how much we pick up just by glancing at people's faces even for a split second.

NON-VERBAL FORMS OF COMMUNICATION

Writing is the most obvious way of sending non-verbal messages. It is important to remember that feedback is more difficult when the message is written. In some cases we can give or get limited feedback; in other cases there is no opportunity for feedback. Letters allow some feedback—you may be able to contact the writer of the letter and ask for further information. Newspaper and magazine articles give you only the opportunity to write a letter to the editor, which may or may not get you more information. Books, of course, don't have any means of giving feedback.

Usually a message will be written at one time and read at a later time. This time lapse alone can cause problems if you don't know when the message was written. For example, you get home from work at 5.30 pm and find a note from your partner which reads, 'Meet me at the shopping centre in an hour'. You have no way of knowing when the note was written, so you don't know what time to be at the shopping centre. And you have no one to ask. In other words, there is no way you can get or give any feedback to the sender. You have to guess what time your partner will be there to meet you. Of course, the situation is not hopeless: you know that you're expected home from work at about 5.30 because that's the time you get home every day. So the note probably means that you should come to the shopping centre one hour after the time that you normally get home.

Another time you come back to your desk at work and find a badly handwritten note telling you about a meeting next Thursday afternoon at 3 pm. The signature at the bottom of the note is impossible to read and you don't recognise the handwriting. You have no idea where the meeting will be held or what it will be about. This communication really doesn't work: you'll just have to wait and see if any more information turns up between now and Thursday.

You can get limited feedback about a book by discussing it with others who have read it. In this way you get at least one other interpretation of the 'message'.

Body language

Body language consists of all the signs and signals we send out by the small movements we make with our faces, the way we sit, stand and move. Although we don't usually realise it, a very large proportion of what we understand comes from our ability to 'read' other people's body language. Do you ever stop to think how you know when the person you are talking to is bored or not interested in what you are saying? Or when they agree with you and feel enthusiastic about your ideas? Do you realise that what you have done when you understand these things, is read the signals they are sending out with such gestures as a nod of the head, a smile, a frown or a shrug of the shoulders?

About 95 per cent of the time we understand those signals more accurately than we understand the words we are hearing. Research by psychologists and sociologists also shows that approximately 80 per cent of our information is taken from body language and about 20 per cent from words. That's why it's so important to listen more carefully on the phone: more than half the message is not getting through!

When you start learning this new language be careful not to interpret single gestures in isolation. Just like any other language, this one has a grammar of its own. Gestures should always be 'read' in clusters: like phrases or sentences. And the context—the situation in which they occur—should also be taken into account. Just as words can change their meanings in different sentences, so gestures can do the same.

Take, for example, the folded arms gesture. It can mean 'I don't like what you're saying. I feel threatened. I'm protecting myself'. Or it may just mean 'I'm in a cold place, in a draught, and I'm trying to keep warm'.

Once we learn to read some of the more common signals we will become better communicators. Instead of being irritated by certain actions we may see them as clues which help us to understand people better.

The way we dress is also a very important part of the message we send to those around us. We all respond most favourably to those people we think are most like us. This is what makes uniforms popular: we all know who you are when you wear any kind of uniform. But even everyday clothing says a lot about us. We can all tell the difference between the boss and the storeman or the mechanic because one of them wears a suit and the others wear overalls, but we can also tell the difference when the signs are less obvious. The important point is that the impression we make will determine the way other people treat us. If Lucy comes to a meeting wearing an Indian skirt, boots and a green mohawk hairdo she can be sure that Mr Porteus, the company accountant, won't take her seriously no matter what she says, unless, perhaps, she works in theatre or advertising.

On the other hand, there is nothing wrong with dressing to suit the situation. We can choose whether we want to belong or 'make a statement'. If we choose to make a statement we have to be prepared to face the consequences: we may be ignored, ridiculed, expelled or not admitted in the first place. If we have achieved a position of influence in a group and then choose to make our statement we have a better chance of being heard.

During the week James is a stockbroker. He wears the suits that stockbrokers wear, with the shoes, shirts and ties that make him instantly recognisable to all the people he meets. On weekends he wears leather jacket and pants, boots and a bike helmet that make him just as easily recognisable as a member of a bikie gang. Neither of these ways of dressing is usually thought of as a uniform, yet they both tell us clearly what 'group' or 'culture' James is operating in. If, eventually, James has some change he would like to bring about in one group with an idea from the other group, he will have a better chance of being heard if he wears the appropriate uniform. Each group will only listen to him if he wears the uniform with which the other members he's talking to are comfortable.

All these elements of communication are important in everyday life, but most of them become more important when we are working in small groups. This is because members of the group become acutely aware of each other's behaviour. Little irritations become magnified. Habits that we would never notice in the ordinary course of events become major problems when we work in close contact with people— just as we know all the good and bad points of the people we live with better than we know anyone we are in contact with only once or twice a week.

And yet, if we care enough about belonging to the group, and we do some careful thinking about the processes that are going on, life in the group can be rewarding. New and interesting experiences will come your way, and you may find that learning to operate in one group will give you skills that will help in other group situations.

CULTURE

Culture is another concept which has an effect on communication. We can define culture as accumulated knowledge based on experiences, meanings, beliefs, biases, attitudes, religions, concepts of self, relationships, and a lot of other things acquired by a large group over many generations. Once we accept this very broad definition we begin to see why and how our culture affects our communication skills. We could say that communication is an important ingredient in culture and culture is an important ingredient in the communication process.

In the next five chapters of this book we will examine many of the notions discussed in this chapter in greater detail.

2

CREATION

THERE ARE MANY types of small group: the first we usually belong to is the family, then there are our friends at school, the sports teams we join, the hobby and interest groups we join, the work groups we find ourselves in, committees we join or perhaps even form, and then some groups we find ourselves taking part in without being sure how we got there—like a jury.

Ideally, a small group has twelve members or fewer so there is always the face-to-face interaction that is needed to build confidence. We can only build up trust and a team spirit with people we know as individuals.

Another important element of a group is that the members share a common goal. When the goal is reached and no new one set, this is no longer true and the group will disintegrate. Even a work team has to satisfy a need for its individual members: this could be just the need to earn wages, or it could be the need to 'belong' or to be productive or recognised. Generally, members have needs which can best be satisfied by participating in group activities. Eventually, if the numbers grow and the group becomes too large for face-to-face interaction, it will split into smaller groups. This brings back the conditions necessary for face-to-face interaction. Another problem which arises when the group is too big is that each member has less time to put forward views. The time allotted in meetings has to be divided among the members and the segments become ever smaller. Goals become fragmented too.

There seems to be a feeling among psychologists and other experts on group behaviour that twelve is a good number of members for a small group. This may be because twelve seems to be the best number for a brainstorming session. When the group is large and not fragmented, then the leader begins to have more influence and meetings can turn into lectures.

Groups are formed in different ways and there are several ways of becoming part of a team. You could be one of the foundation members, invited to join a team which is being formed; you may change your job and find that you are automatically included in a group which already exists; you could be invited to join an existing team to replace someone who has left; or perhaps you could be asked to form a team to perform some special task. Each way of joining makes different demands on you in regard to the way you present yourself and the impression you will make on others.

The processes, for the group as a whole, will follow the path explained in this and the following chapters. The level of participation in some of those processes will vary between group members.

These days many companies are creating work teams in an effort to improve productivity. Instead of production lines, with operators performing routine tasks, workers are being asked to take on the responsibility of the entire process. One of the most important aspects of this practice is that it leads to multiskilling. Team members learn new skills which are usually transportable: you take the new knowledge with you when you move on to a new team or a new job.

This brings us to the next possibility: you change your job and find that you have to fit into a team which already exists. This is easier than joining a group as a foundation member, but you'll still need to learn something. The problems of fitting in are slightly different to those of becoming part of a new group and we will discuss them under the headings 'Tolerance' and 'Emotions'.

Another way of becoming part of a group is to replace someone who, for one reason or another, has left the group. This can be tricky because the group might feel that you don't quite measure up to the person you are replacing, or the opposite could happen, and the person who left was so bad that you have to prove that you are better. Either way, it is up to you to make an effort to fit in.

One other way of becoming part of a group is through an invitation or direction to form it. The surest way to get into this situation is to make suggestions at meetings about things which need improvement. You may be asked to form a committee or task group to look into or deal with a matter.

For example, Jack noticed that there was a powdery substance falling from the ceiling in one area of the office. He asked a few people what it could be and then sent a sample off to a friend in a laboratory for analysis. It turned out to be asbestos and Jack was asked by his colleagues to organise a work team to look into the problems it might be causing. The team collected information on the hazards of asbestos and on methods of removal, then came up with a plan for carrying out the work with the minimum of disruption. They handed all the information over to management and the team disbanded.

Once you have the necessary skills you will find opportunities to form teams of your own when you believe some action must be taken. Once you have experience of working on a team you may, in fact, be ready and willing to take on this type of activity.

ASSERTIVENESS

In every communication we have three distinct choices of how to behave: we can be assertive, non-assertive or aggressive.

Non-assertive behaviour can take several different forms. We sometimes mistake non-assertiveness for politeness. We don't want to upset the other person, so we don't state our own feelings or opinions in case they don't match the other person's feelings or beliefs. Quite often, though, when we think we are being polite we are storing a grievance away for later use.

Salesman: (At door) Good morning, Ma'am. Your house has been chosen for a special offer we have. We'll put a brand new roof on your house for the cost of materials only. All we ask in return is that we be allowed to use your house in our advertising.

Householder: Well, it sounds very interesting, but . . .

Salesman: I'm sure you and your husband will be pleased with our offer.

Unless this woman stops being polite and gets rid of the salesman she is very likely to feel resentful later.

Another way of being non-assertive is by not speaking up when we feel that we don't have any rights. We may feel that we don't have the right to express our feelings. For example, someone in a higher position than us—a supervisor, a manager—hurts our feelings or makes us angry, but we don't believe that we have the right to express that anger. Sometimes we feel that we don't even have the right to be angry.

Some people behave in a non-assertive manner because they are afraid of what will happen if they are assertive. They are fearful of losing the approval of those around them. They are also worried about sounding stupid or selfish or hurting other people's feelings.

Ted: When you get there, tell them that you'll go to Consumer Affairs if they don't fix it right away.

Alec: (Has no intention of saying that but doesn't want to sound weak in front of Ted) Yes, yes.

Ted: And don't forget to tell them that you only bought it last week.

Being non-assertive may make for an easy life, but in the long run it doesn't gain us any respect unless we do it carefully. This doesn't mean that we should never be non-assertive: there are times when it can be very useful to be polite, to put our own interests aside in favour of the group, or to prevent another person from feeling foolish or inadequate. We should be aware, though, of what we are doing.

Aggressive behaviour, like non-assertive behaviour, has its place, but not in everyday dealings with people we want to have an ongoing relationship with. Aggressive behaviour tends to antagonise those who come in contact with it, especially if we are aggressive all the time.

We often behave in an aggressive way when we feel threatened—when we feel that other people are attacking us either physically or verbally. They may simply be behaving in an assertive manner, but if they do it too often we may respond by becoming aggressive just to stop ourselves from being non-assertive.

Sometimes aggression is the result of previous unpleasant experiences. We may have found in the past that our assertive statements were not listened to, and that the only way to be heard was to become aggressive. The aggressive behaviour pattern can become a habit, and certain subjects will trigger the aggression.

For example, every time Edna said she wanted to go to the movies, Joe ignored her and they went to the pub instead. This went on for years. Eventually the time came when Edna had had enough. The next time she wanted to go to the movies, instead of being assertive she became mildly aggressive and it worked. But Joe wasn't going to fall for the same thing twice, so when Edna tried it again she had to be a little more aggressive. It got to the stage where Joe was taking her to the movies just to avoid the aggressive behaviour. Trouble was, he was building up a terrific reservoir of resentment.

There are some people who believe that the only way to get anything worthwhile is by being aggressive. And there are those who have never learnt assertive behaviour patterns and think that aggression is the only alternative to non-assertive behaviour.

Assertiveness basically means saying your piece in a non-threatening manner and making your intentions and your needs clear without threatening anyone else. In order to be assertive we need to look at some aspects of our personalities. Are we happy with ourselves? Do we have sufficient self-esteem? Do we feel comfortable asking for our rights? Do we know what our rights are?

Your first right is to be able to be yourself, take responsibility for your own actions and judge your own thoughts, feelings and behaviour. Taking this one step further, you have the right to voice your opinion and say what you think and believe, even when other people disagree with you. What we are talking about when we discuss assertiveness is the way you say things rather than what you say.

Using 'I-language' is an important part of assertiveness. 'I-language' expresses our thoughts without judging the people we're talking to or their opinions or actions. For example:

Patsy: You must be deaf if you have to play the stereo so loud.

Basil: I'm not deaf. I just like it like that.

Compare this approach

Patsy: When the stereo is so loud I feel as if I'm being
                punched in the head, and I don't like that.
Basil: Would you like to have the volume turned down?

By stating our position and needs we are more likely to have a sensible discussion. The other person won't feel threatened and will be more likely to consider our request.

Because assertiveness is such an important aspect of communication it will come up again later.

SELF-ESTEEM

Your self-esteem is the way you feel about yourself. When you are happy with what you are and with the way you perform, your self-esteem will be high. And when you feel good about yourself you will feel good about everyone around you too. Don't send self-defeating messages to yourself. Instead of saying, 'I never remember all the things I have to do', try telling yourself, 'I can make a list in a diary of the things I have to do each day'.

Think of some of your own self-defeating messages, and see if you can reverse them so they become positive messages instead. It's a good idea to keep a small notebook handy for a day or two. Jot down all the negative messages you send yourself. At the end of the time, read through them and write down positive messages to take the place of each of the negative ones. Having written them down you are more likely to remember them and also more likely to use them in the future. It does take practice, but it's amazing what you can do when you don't know what you can't do.

A good way to build your self-esteem is by keeping track of even the smallest successes you have each day. Set yourself small goals that are achievable: if you usually sleep in and then have to rush, try getting up on time just once. When you achieve this, try it again. Then try for another small achievement. Be nice to your mother-in-law when she phones. Once you've been successful, give yourself Brownie points. Promise yourself something special—a new book, tickets to a game or a show—whatever you consider a treat. The best way to build your self-esteem is by getting onto the success spiral. The more you achieve, the more successful you'll be and the better you'll like yourself.

TOLERANCE

One of the most important feelings we have is that of wanting to belong. When we join a new group we usually try hard to fit in. Caution makes us try harder to be polite, say the right things, avoid any conflict. Anything that could upset others is carefully avoided. Well, most of us are like that. There are some people who don't care and don't take any notice of other people's feelings. They are intolerant. Other attitudes which get in the way during the early stages of group formation are prejudice and bigotry.

We are prejudiced when we make assumptions about other people before we really get to know them. For instance, we may think that all people with red hair have quick tempers or—common misconception these days—that all blondes are stupid. These ideas, as well as being wrong, can also be very hurtful to the person concerned.

Bigotry is just as bad: it is the belief that only our own moral code and behaviour are acceptable and that anything different that anyone else believes is wrong. For example, we get upset about people who eat snakes or frogs and yet have difficulty understanding why others would be upset because we eat cows or pigs. There is nothing more 'right' about eating any one of these than any other.

EMOTIONS

We seldom talk about our feelings. It is difficult to discuss our anger, irritation or boredom and for most of us it is even hard to talk about excitement and affection. Because of this difficulty we usually show our emotions in other ways.

Anger usually shows in our faces. Our eyes close to slits, our mouths become straight, tight-lipped lines, and our jaws and necks may become tense. Irritation is another feeling we all recognise instinctively: the pencil, finger or foot tapping; the fidgeting with rings, watch, clothing, the attempts at interruption. Think about your own ways of signalling these feelings.

Boredom is another state of mind we recognise easily, even when the other person is trying to cover up. Yawns can be discreetly hidden behind a hand, but boredom will still show in a person's eyes: they become glazed, unfocussed and you know you've lost your listener. This is why body language is so important.

We learn very early in life to understand the signs of anger and annoyance, but we also learn the signals for happiness and approval. Once we understand more about both body language and assertiveness we will be better able to deal not only with our own emotions but also with those displayed by other people in our group. Another bonus of working in an ongoing group is that as we become familiar with the other group members, we become better at understanding their emotions and their behaviour patterns.

In the beginning, while the group members are still getting to know one another, there will be some anxiety about hurting other people's feelings. We will be nervous about displaying our own emotions, especially enthusiasm or excitement because we all fear being ridiculed. It will take some time for members of the group to reach the stage where they feel comfortable enough with each other to let their true emotions show.

However, this is one area of learning which will help you the next time you join a group. People really have a limited number of emotions which they display in public. The more you learn about how they are signalled the easier it becomes to read them. Eventually you'll read them instinctively and, in time, become known as a good 'people person'.

PERCEPTION

Perception is the way we see things. Because we have all had different experiences, come from different backgrounds and have a variety of expectations, we see the same thing in different ways. To get an idea of what this means in practice imagine yourself in the following ways:

- as you see yourself;
- as your husband/wife/lover sees you;

- as your parents/children see you;
- as your boss sees you;
- as your doctor sees you.

This list could go on for quite a while and, if you are honest with yourself, you'll realise that each of these people sees you differently. Just one example: your parents will usually 'see' you as much younger than you 'see' yourself and your children will 'see' you as much older than you do. So perception is the point from which you are viewing things. And just because you and I have had the same experiences, doesn't mean we will see a situation in the same way. There are far too many factors which combine to create our particular viewpoint.

What does happen, though, is that we become attached to people with whom we feel we have a lot in common. We then spend a lot of time with them, share experiences with them, discuss and influence one another's reactions and become closer in our respective perceptions of situations. This is why couples who have been together for many years often think and act alike.

LEADERSHIP

It would be difficult to say exactly which qualities are needed in a leader. Intelligence and sensitivity are certainly important, but it is impossible to guarantee that anything in particular will make for effective leadership in all situations.

Many groups will, in fact, have two leaders: a formal one and an informal one. One of these will be the task leader, the other will be the social–emotional leader. There is no fixed rule about whether the task leader will be the formal or informal leader.

The task leader is the person who has some expertise in the work the group is doing. If the group has been formed to organise an art show to raise money for the local school, then the task leader will be someone who has done this before. It could be a local artist; it could be a parent who has connections in the art world; it could be someone who is a good organiser.

The social–emotional leader is the person who can pour oil on troubled waters. This person will have skills in conflict resolution, perhaps in counselling, in communication and will be a 'people person' who gets people working together, gets things done and keeps everyone happy and contented.

The formal leader is the person who is accepted by the group as such. This is the person who chairs meetings and acts as spokesperson and representative of the group to the outside world. The informal leader is the one who takes control in those situations where the accepted leader doesn't do so well.

Let's look for a moment at these dualities: task leader/social-emotional leader; formal/informal leader. Quite often in a long-term group the formal leader will be a people person and the informal leader will emerge as tasks change. In fact in small groups of an ongoing nature, the task leadership will change. And this is as it should be, because the change in leadership should be related to the task the group is working on. Provided there is confidence, trust and affection between members, this change is easily accomplished and is good for the group. It gives everyone the confidence to realise that they could also, when the opportunity presents itself, become a group leader.

What we have to realise is that mostly the situation determines the leader. The person who is a good leader in one situation, or for one group, is not necessarily a good leader under different conditions. In one group the leader will need to be a caring, concerned person who will look after people and possessions. In another the leader may need to be a ruthless bully. For example, it wouldn't be any good having an aggressive, shouting authoritarian as the leader of a social group which arranges the monthly church get-together. But that is just the sort of person you might choose to be a drill sergeant. If the situation needs aggression, an aggressive person will emerge. For a situation which needs patience, there will be a calm, patient person.

BASIC MEETING PROCEDURES

Meetings can so easily turn into a waste of everybody's time. To make them effective we need to plan them carefully, inform everyone who will attend what the meeting will be about, structure the time and ensure that proper records are kept.

Planning the meeting consists not only of arranging a suitable place and time for the meeting and informing the necessary people that they will need to be there, but also in preparing an agenda. A well-written agenda lists all the topics or items which will be discussed, it states the approximate amount of time which has been allocated to each item and it also shows who is in charge of the project. This alerts people to any responsibilities they may have to bring information to the meeting so that the group can make decisions. It also lets them know how long the topic will be under discussion and at what stage of the meeting the matter is likely to be brought up. Obviously, the agenda should not be so rigid that change cannot occur, and you should allow for the possibility that one or other item on the agenda may run for more or less time than was originally allocated. But you need to beware that this doesn't happen too often.

People need to be told well enough in advance when the meeting is to be held to lessen the likelihood that they will have already made other appointments for that time. The agenda needs to be handed to everyone—but especially to those who have to bring information to the meeting—in good time for them to think about the issues to be discussed. Two or three days before the meeting is usually enough time for people to give the matters some thought and perhaps make some notes.

Before the meeting begins you need to arrange for one member of the group to take notes. This can be anyone who is able to summarise the discussion and write down key points. The other information that needs to be noted during the meeting are the names of the people who will be responsible for any action which needs to be taken on any issue before the next meeting. This information will be needed for the next agenda. In chapter 3 we will discuss agendas in more detail. You'll also find some sample agendas there.

CASE STUDY

Favourite Pickle Manufacturers have decided to try the team approach in a small way. If the first team proves successful they will form other teams in other areas of their operation. Eight people have been invited to join the team. For this first meeting, the venue was booked by the Personnel Officer and everyone was notified that the meeting would take place at 11.30 am. At this meeting some of the foundation members know one another and some have only seen each other once or twice. At present all they have in common is that they all work for the same company.

Susie, from Accounts, is first to arrive, about five minutes before the meeting is due to start. She enters the room and sits halfway along the far side of the table, putting her notepad and pencils in front of her. Next to arrive is Peter. He takes the seat at the head of the table and leans back.

Peter:	Have you organised tea and coffee?
Susie:	(Looking a little surprised) No.
Peter:	Well don't you think you should?
Susie:	No. Why? (Then adds): I had my morning tea break at ten.
Peter:	What are you here for?

Before Susie can reply, several more people enter the room including Steve, the Personnel Officer, who organised the meeting. He goes to the chair at the opposite end of the table from Peter. Everyone else sits down, shuffles about for a minute and then settles down. Peter is leaning back in his chair, hands clasped behind his head, looking at the people round the table.

Peter:	(As soon as there is silence) Let's get this thing over so we can get back to work.
Susie:	I thought this was going to be a long-term project . . .

She doesn't sound too sure. She can't help believing that Peter must have some information she hasn't been given. After all, she reasons, he's a supervisor in the factory and she's a clerk in the Accounts section: he probably knows much more than she does. Susie's perception of what a supervisor is and does is evident in her behaviour.

Steve:	Well, I did tell you that this would be a preliminary meeting. Just to discuss how the group will operate and what you'll be expected to do.

Steve is not the most forceful person at the meeting: he speaks quite softly, sits on the edge of the chair and clasps his hands on the table. His body language is defensive.

Peter:	I don't have time to muck about here. This agenda you sent says we have to choose a group leader. Well, let's get on with it then.
Steve:	First I'd like to explain to everyone what the group will be doing.
Margaret:	Is this going to keep us away from our usual work very much?

Margaret is a leading hand in the Labelling section of the factory. She doesn't like Peter very much—she finds him bossy and chauvinistic. Also she finds Susie a bit intimidating: Margaret feels that people look down on her because she doesn't read and write as well as Susie. Margaret's perception of herself doesn't necessarily match the perception others have of her. Before the meeting she had a long chat with Steve, to find out as much as she could about what would be expected from the group. She already knows the answer to her question, but wants Steve to make it clear to the group, especially to Peter.

Steve:	Yes, you'll have to make sure that there is someone who can take your place while you are working on the group project as well as when you're at a meeting.
Peter:	(Glaring at Steve) I don't have anyone who can take my place.
Steve:	Who does your work when you're off sick?
Peter:	I'm never sick.
Steve:	We may have to look at putting someone else in your place on this team until you train somebody to take over your job when you aren't there.

Susie, who has been listening to this conversation quite carefully, notices a look of fear on Peter's face. The look only lasts a moment and is gone, and then Peter is back to his usual pompous self. Susie's perceptiveness—the fact that she is noticing things about others—will help her later.

| Wendy: | What are we supposed to be doing here anyway? |
| Peter: | (Impatiently) Yes, what do we have to do? |

Steve tells the group about the company decision to try teamwork on a small scale.

Steve: As a trial the boss wants the group to look at health and safety issues in the factory. You'll have to see what is happening and how things can be improved. How you do that is up to the group. Personnel will be there if you feel that any or all of you need help.

Steve looks around the group. Everyone is listening but no one has anything to say.

Steve: You'll have to choose a group leader and someone who'll take notes at each meeting and be responsible for keeping the records.

Wendy: Why don't you just choose a leader for us?

Steve: Because the group has to be happy with the choice. So it's better for the group to choose the leader themselves. You could do it by a show of hands or you could each say what experience you have had that would help you to be the leader.

Peter: Well, I reckon I should be the leader. I'm the most senior one here.

Two or three people murmur agreement.

Margaret: But you said you couldn't leave your job because you had no one to take your place.

Peter: Yeah, well, I could organise something, I s'pose.

Steve: Is there anyone else who feels they would like to be the group leader?

Margaret: (Firmly) I would like to have a go at it. (One element of her decision may be to avoid having to take notes.)

Peter: (Loudly) What would you know about it?

Margaret: I've been a Guide leader for a long time. I'm a leading hand in my section and I've been running a household with four kids for the last fifteen years.

Steve: As I said, it's not for me to choose a leader for you. What I suggest is that the members should vote for Peter or Margaret. D'you want to have an open vote or a secret one?

The characters—some analysis

Susie is ambitious. She is a unit leader in the Accounts department. She is responsible for allocating work to several clerks and ensuring that this work is done. She is efficient, quietly spoken and a good listener. As a leader Susie would find it difficult to deal with someone like Peter, mainly because she doesn't have experience with his personality type. Apart from this she would be a good choice as leader.

Peter is considerably older than the other members of this group. He has been a supervisor on the factory floor for a long time. Although he is respected by the management, his workers don't like him quite as much. He believes that women are only meant to do things like make tea and coffee or work on process lines because 'they can't think things through'. In fact, he really thinks they shouldn't work at all—they should be home cooking and cleaning. He feels that he is the only possible person to be the leader of this group. It will be extremely difficult for him to work effectively within the group if a woman is the leader. On the other hand, he is acutely aware that his age is against him in the work force. Having been a supervisor for a long time and not having had any further promotion, he realises that he is likely to be offered early retirement unless he can adapt to this new way of working.

If Margaret and Susie are able to show him that he will be respected if he tries to change his attitude, he may remain in the group. It is possible, though, that he is too set in his thinking to be able to change, and will end up leaving the group.

Margaret has come back into the workforce after fifteen years of raising kids. She is a caring sort of person and within a few months of starting work was given the position of leading hand. She is responsible for the operation of a machine and supervises two other workers in the Labelling section. At first her self-esteem was rather low and she was frightened of seeming stupid. With some help from Steve and other Personnel staff, she has gained confidence and is now quite happy to be joining this group. She has a little trouble dealing with Peter: he is too much like her husband!

Wendy has also recently returned to the workforce. Her children are still very young and are left in a day-care centre while she is at work. She is nervous, insecure and even, at times, frightened. Her greatest fear is that she will lose her job. She works in Peter's section and finds him intimidating.

Peter's behaviour toward Susie before the meeting is not acceptable. He seems to think that her function is to make tea or coffee for the people attending. He is going to find it difficult to cope with the fact that the group will be predominantly female. His body language—when he puts his hands behind his head and leans back in the chair—shows that he looks down on the rest of the group. Susie is confident enough to respond assertively. She uses a pleasant manner and simply states her facts. What do you think Peter may have said if Steve hadn't walked in when he did? Or Susie? It is very likely that Steve prevented an argument. Peter is the sort of person who believes that men should be making all the decisions. Steve, on the other hand, believes that women should be given more opportunities and that there should be more women in top positions. Not everyone feels as strongly as Peter and we need to learn to distinguish between different degrees of feelings and beliefs that people hold.

Getting to the next stage—conflict

Before the group is ready to go on to the next stage of its growth as a unit, it will have to deal with some of the problems it is experiencing. The members will have to get to know one another well enough to choose a leader. They will have to learn about each other. Roles will be taken up and members will begin to understand their relationship to other members. During this growth period, the members will begin to formulate group goals and problems to be dealt with.

Most of the problems we have discussed will have to be resolved for the next stage to run smoothly. That is not to say that all the problems will be solved. Some problems will probably remain with the group for its entire life and those are the kinds of things that we all have to learn to live with. This is tolerance—learning to live in a less than perfect world.

The group at the pickle factory has been formed by someone else in the company. The people who now make up the group probably would have chosen a different set of members. We usually choose to work with people we already know. It's always hard work getting to know new people.

Looking at the information that Steve has given our group, we know that the members have to decide for themselves—as a group—what issue they will tackle first. They have only had the suggestion that it should be in the health and safety area of operations. The group, in a fairly short time, will have to ask and answer such questions as: What is the task? How will we choose which task we will work on? Who is the group leader? Is the group in complete agreement about this? How well do members relate to one another? Once these questions are answered the group will be able to decide how to fulfil its role; what precise problem or problems it will work on; and how it will solve them.

The 'conflict' becomes worse when the group has been created by management. When a group is formed spontaneously because the members have a common goal or common needs, a lot of these questions won't arise.

This first stage in the life of a group can, and often does, last through several meetings, as members become more familiar with each other as well as with the workings of the group and the job to be tackled. Bear in mind, though, that not all groups are task-oriented: some, like a bridge club, a book club or a rock band, are formed around common interests.

Before the group can start working on the actual problem it will deal with, it will have to sort out the leadership issue. Because the group is small, it's important that everyone in it should feel comfortable with the leader. No one should be frightened or intimidated by the leader. Peter is rather pushy—we have already heard that he sees himself as the logical choice for leader—and Wendy and others are afraid of losing their jobs. Maria also knows Peter but works in another section. Probably the only person in the group who is not intimidated by Peter is Susie. She is also the only person who noticed Peter's fear.

Wendy offers to be the secretary after she learns that this will mean taking notes at the meetings, keeping written records of everything the group does or decides, writing the agenda and calling the meetings.

Meanwhile, Margaret, who has assumed temporary leadership, asks the group members to think about the problems they could work on.

The group decides to close this first meeting and meet again in three days time. By then everyone is expected to have looked around their area and consulted their workmates so they can come to the next meeting with some suggestions of problems which could be looked into.

BEING OBSERVANT

When we look at the same things over and over, day after day, we get to a stage where we no longer really see them: they blend into the background and become just another part of the scenery. A similar situation comes about when we live or work near a railway line or a busy road: after a while we no longer hear the trains or the traffic until someone reminds us of them.

Once we learn to look at things 'with our eyes wide open' we begin to see things from a new point of view. And if we also start to ask 'why?' we will begin to understand that most areas in our working lives can be improved. A bonus is that people work better when they understand why they are performing a certain task. Being observant could be defined as 'seeing and understanding'.

RISK-TAKING

In order to go on to the next stage, we also need to take some risks: we need to put our point of view forward, even though our ideas may be ridiculed by other members of the group. As a group we need to learn to listen to each other's points of view without making judgements, at least in the early stages. Once we can do this we will also be prepared to put our own views forward, knowing that they will be accepted by the group in the same way we accept other members' views. This is not always as easy as it sounds: we become very attached to our ideas, we feel that they are somehow a part of us and when someone attacks our ideas we feel as though they are having a go at us personally. In order to be ready for the next stage of the group function we need to overcome this feeling of risk.

A good way to stop feeling anxious about this risk is to try to have as many ideas as possible. That way, when one idea is not so good, you still have others to try out.

The stages we talk about in this book show the ideal growth pattern for a group. This is rarely achieved exactly as we see it here. We must realise that any group is made up of a collection of individuals and that we are all unique. Putting several individuals together and expecting things to run smoothly from the beginning, then all the way through the group process, is completely unrealistic. The group can meet problems at any stage and some groups have problems at every stage. How well they cope, whether they overcome the difficulties and the group survives to the end of the project, depends very much on the combination of personalities. Sometimes the addition or subtraction of just one person can make a tremendous difference to the functioning of the group.

The growth from one stage to another is not usually something which will be noticeable—it's not like crossing a border and getting a stamp in your passport, or passing from one school year into another and getting a progress report. The transition will be gradual and unless you are particularly looking for the signs described here, the group should be relatively unaware of having gone from one stage to the next. Information in the following chapters will help you identify which stage the group is in so you can find solutions to the problems your group is experiencing.

The group will have moved from the first stage when members are willing to risk the possibility of some conflict. They will have stopped using 'polite' non-assertive language and be willing to take on tasks and topics which could lead to differences of opinion.

Members will have stopped discussing the group's purpose and will have made a commitment to it even if they do not completely agree with it. This means that the group will be able to concentrate on the task—content—rather than on the process. Members will be prepared to risk the personal attacks which they realise may occur once everyone stops being so polite. Not that politeness is wrong, but most of us are overly polite when we feel unfamiliar with the other people in the group. Once we become more familiar we tend to relax and are then more likely to speak our minds. It is this openness which can make us feel as if we are being attacked.

3

CONFLICT

THE SECOND STAGE, which some groups reach by the third meeting and some groups never reach, is marked by conflict relating to power, criticism and stress. So this section will look closely at these topics.

If power struggles are not resolved in this stage then the group will not survive in its present form. But the problems which arise in this stage are usually the most difficult to resolve. Most of the solutions will need some changes of behaviour on the part of one or more group members. Some groups have required all members to make some changes to their way of operating.

One of the first difficulties which arises is that we have all been conditioned by society, by our education, to be competitive. This is fine for the group as a whole, especially if it is only one of a number of groups within the same company, or a sports team which is competing with other teams. But for the individuals who make up the team or group it is no good competing against one another within the group. So we have, as individuals, to be non-competitve—cooperative—within the group but competitive as a group in relation to other groups. In order for this to happen it is vital to develop a team spirit, a feeling of unity within the group. And this is why the power struggles which take place at this stage need to be resolved for the group to begin concentrating on its tasks.

With regard to content, members will want to know, at this stage, about operating rules for the group, who sets the agenda and who decides which tasks the group will work on and when. Members will also ask what, if any, limits there are on the group's authority, finances and resources. They will also want to know how they will be assessed, how their work will be evaluated and to whom they are answerable.

Because most of these topics have equal importance in this stage we will first look at those which are task-related and then those which are concerned with process.

PREPARING AN AGENDA

The agenda for a meeting is like the program for a concert: it lists the items in the order in which they will occur. But before we can prepare the agenda (or the program) we need to find out what members want to talk about. Some of this information will come from the last meeting, and some of it will come from the activities of group members between meetings.

If you are preparing the agenda you'll need to contact the people expected to be at the meeting and find out if they have any items that will need to be listed on it. If you are one of the members and want something discussed at the next meeting, you should contact the person responsible for the agenda and let them know what you want to present and how much time you think you will need.

A well written agenda should look like this.

MEETING OF MARGARET'S TEAM

11 am, Tuesday 15 March

Training Room A

Minutes of previous meeting	5mins	Wendy
Report on installation of new machine	5mins	Peter
Progress report on repairs to air-conditioning unit in factory	2mins	Xuan
Discussion of ideas for re-organisation of tracking of orders	15mins	All
General business	3mins	All

This agenda is for a half-hour meeting which will probably run to about forty minutes. One reason meetings usually run overtime is that most of us have trouble judging how long two or three minutes really is. So, though Xuan has two minutes in which to give his report on the air-conditioning repairs, if anyone asks a question or makes any comment on his report it will take a bit longer. We could make allowance for this in the time we give him, but that may make him think he has to talk for longer. If he only needs to tell us what progress, if any, has been made, then giving him more time might make him feel that he has to find more information.

On the other hand, having given Peter five minutes to talk about the installation of the new machine, we can easily tell him, when he goes on for almost ten minutes, that he will have to finish off as we have other matters to attend to. And we can do it without feeling guilty and without him feeling as if we were attacking him personally.

Meetings in the workplace should always be kept as short and informative as possible. The meeting is not our job—only an important part of it. This means that we can't do without them, but we shouldn't let them become the only thing we do. After all, if we spend our whole working day in meetings we'll have to take work home with us or stay back late to get things done.

Let's look now at a different kind of agenda. This one is for the committee of a local sports club.

DELTA SPORTS CLUB

Meeting to be held on Tuesday 15 March at 7.30 pm in the clubhouse

1	Minutes of previous meeting (15 Feb)	5mins	EB
2	Correspondence	5mins	EB
3	Treasurer's report	5mins	AL
4	State competition	5mins	RG
5	Fundraising—cake stall)		PM
	—fete)	20mins	LH
	—car wash)		WJ
6	Business arising	5min	
7	General		WJ, SR & AL

As you can see, at this meeting someone—probably the secretary—will read out the minutes of the previous meeting and will also read any letters which have been received or sent out on the committee's behalf. Let's now look at the way time has been allotted in both these agendas. Routine business, in both cases, has been given only a few minutes. These things, like accepting the minutes of the previous meeting, have to be done to keep everything tidy, but they shouldn't be given too much time. They don't move the action along. But those items which are of most importance, and those to which we give the largest chunk of time, shouldn't come too early in the meeting. There are several reasons for this. First of all, we need to allow people to settle into the mood of the meeting. Secondly, if we schedule the important items too early in the meeting, the discussion may become heated and matters won't be resolved as quickly as they could be. The meeting will then go over time or people will leave at the end of the time they allowed. Either way, the normal routine business will not be dealt with properly.

There are videos available from most libraries on meeting procedures—many of them amusing as well as informative, especially the John Cleese films *Meetings Bloody Meetings* and *More Bloody Meetings*.

EVALUATION

What the team does and how it functions will depend to a large extent on some external factors. One of these is evaluation. By whom and how will the work of the team be evaluated? In business the time the team spends on projects needs to be cost-effective. This means that there must be some benefit to the company. For example, a team may show that what it has suggested will save the company money, or will produce more income. For example, improving work practices in an area could save the company money, or adding an extra product line without much expenditure could lead to added revenue. With a sports team it's also quite easy to evaluate results: everyone from the coach and the manager to the last fan knows whether the team is winning or losing.

With some other groups, though, it is more difficult to decide if they are successful or not. A non-profit group whose purpose is to organise social functions for members of the community to get to know each other better will be judged differently by different people. The members of the small group may feel they are successful when they get a good attendance at a dance. The people who come to the dance may judge how successful it was by the music: if they liked the music it was a good dance, if they didn't, it wasn't. The community management may decide that the dance was a success if the ticket sales covered expenses. If there was a shortfall, and money had to be taken from elsewhere to pay the expenses, the dance may be considered a failure.

So, when we look at an evaluation of some activity we need to know who was responsible for the report and the criteria they used.

RULES

In this stage of the group process we are likely to ask questions about rules affecting our group's activities. We need to know what we are expected to do, how we are to do our work, how much time we have, what resources are available, and a lot of other information before we can go about the tasks we have been given.

Just as there are rules about how to run a meeting, there are rules about everything else we do. We know instinctively that the rules for running a meeting are different to the rules of behaviour which operate at a social gathering. Some rules apply in all situations: for example, we all recognise courtesy and respect as acceptable behaviour wherever we are.

In this stage of the life of the group we need some rules to be stated so that we can get on with the business of the task in hand. So we need to look to management for the answers to such questions as:

- How much time does the group have in which to come to some conclusions?
- Is the group responsible for implementing the changes suggested?
- To whom is the group answerable?
- Who will give approval for expenditure of money?
- Who will give support when the group meets opposition in the workplace?

With a little thought the group should be able to come up with more questions of this nature. These questions should be answered by management, or by the group itself, before the group goes any further into the task. Without setting up ground rules such as these, the group could easily get enthusiastic about its task only to find that nothing comes of all its work because there is no money to fund the recommended changes, or because the ideas have not been presented to the right people, or for a number of other reasons which could have been prevented by clearly establishing the rules before the game started. After all, no team goes into a game without first knowing the rules.

Other rules which should be decided on at the beginning of the group's life concern such issues as the distribution of workload, codes of behaviour, and anything else which may cause problems later. If discussion of these kinds of rules is left for later 'when the matter comes up', there could be debate as group members take sides and defend or accuse each other. Of course, not every eventuality can be foreseen, but it is worthwhile to have a brainstorming session on the topic of rules.

QUESTIONING TECHNIQUES

Questions can be divided roughly into two groups: open questions and closed questions.

Closed questions are those that need only short answers, like 'yes', 'no' or 'I don't know'. They are useful when we need a quick answer to something we think we know. 'Are you going to the Post Office?' 'You know you should be here by 8.30, don't you?' 'Do you want a cup of coffee?'

When we really want more information than just a 'yes' or 'no' we need to ask open questions. They invite the other person to give us more information. Instead of asking 'Is the house white?' ask 'What does the house look like?' or even 'What colour is the house?' This last question will get a shorter answer than the one before it, but will probably get a longer answer than the first question.

It takes practice to ask open questions. One way to make your questions more open is to begin them with words like what, where, how, when, why or who. Questions which begin with the words 'do', 'don't', 'will' or 'won't' are usually closed.

We don't need to make all our questions open ones. We just need to be aware of the information we need before we ask them. If we need confirmation of information we already have, then we can ask closed questions. To collect more information we need to ask open questions.

STATUS

No matter how much we believe that everyone is equal we have to realise that within any group there will be a natural order. Most large organisations are shaped like a pyramid with a leader at the top and all the other members forming the layers below that.

In a small group we may find that the structure is flat: there is a leader and below that all members are equal. This would be the ideal situation for a small group because the leader would not have total power as long as the group can change its leader whenever it wants.

Even when leadership can change we mostly 'know our place'. We instinctively consider some members to be superior to us, some to be our equals and others to be inferior. What we don't seem to consider very often is that this perception changes, depending on the circumstances. We may be a leader in one situation and at the 'bottom of the heap' in another. Take, for example, Xuan. At work he is near the bottom of the ladder—he operates a machine. In his religious community he is an elder, the equivalent of a 'middle manager' in a business community; in his ethnic community he is on the board of the local social club and helps new migrants with housing problems— his qualifications as a mechanical engineer give him high status.

Margaret has a similar situation. At work she has a fairly low status job but in her spare time she is the chairwoman of the local Girl Guide division and is very highly respected in Guiding circles.

Think about your own status in different areas of your life: when we are young or very old we feel that our families don't hold us in very high esteem but in other places things are different. The young person is perhaps very popular and respected in a sporting community. An older person may command far more respect at work or in a social group than at home.

COMMITMENT

This stage—conflict—is when members of the group make a commitment. If they are not prepared to do so, there is little point in them remaining in the group. Without the commitment of every member the group's work will fail. In our case study in chapter 2 the team must either get a commitment from Peter or it must ensure that Peter leaves the group. If he stays in the group without this commitment he will constantly undermine its efforts. When he is asked to do something he will usually accept the task allocated but will not deliver. His excuses will always come later, when it is time to present information or produce something, and this will then hold up the work of other members of the group. This is passive resistance and is far worse than having someone who admits from the start that they are not interested in doing their share. The person who is honest about their lack of commitment will usually withdraw of their own accord. It is the person who wants to belong without making a commitment who is the problem.

ROLES

We all have different roles which we play. This is not to say that we are not sincere or serious: most of our roles are very serious. We are, at different stages of our lives, different things to different people. At any given time you may be a parent, a child, a student, a teacher, a worker, a member of a sports team, a customer, a friend, etc. In each of these roles we behave slightly differently. We do this without conscious thought. This is partly in response to the way we are treated when another person starts the conversation. If the teacher walks into the room and addresses the people as students then, even if they are all adults, they will respond in the way that they know students should respond. Of course, individual people will respond in ways which they learned when they were school students, but there will be enough similarities for them to realise that they are all students. We also know, from our experience, how to behave in the other roles mentioned earlier. Customers behave in certain ways, workers are aware of the behaviour expected from them, and so on.

When we become part of a group, we may need to learn some new behaviour patterns. We have to realise that we need to be supportive of other group members' opinions. When we learn to do this, we will find that the other members respond in a similar way: they become supportive of us and our opinions. Cooperation is another skill we need to practise.

One role that we see in group behaviour, which is not as easily recognisable in other situations, is that of the clarifier. This person feels it is their job to make sure that everyone understands everything that everyone else has said. Unless there actually are members in the group who don't understand—for whatever reason—this person can drive everyone mad. On the other hand, there may be a group member who doesn't speak very good English, or who is deaf or for whom the jargon is really new and strange and in this case the clarifier will be highly valued.

There will probably also be someone in the group who feels that they need to ask questions for everyone. This person usually believes, at least subconsciously, that the other people in the group may not understand everything that is happening, so they ask questions which they think the others should have asked. If you think this is happening and it is annoying the group, you could simply ask the person whether they know the answer to the question they are asking. If they know the answer you can point out that everyone else does, too. If they don't have the answers you have to assume that they really need to ask the questions. In this case you just have to be patient and ensure that information is given more clearly.

There are some roles which people take on without meaning to do so. One of these is the person who works better on their own. They may become quarrelsome when working with a group. Or they may withdraw, physically or mentally. A good way to deal with them is to give them tasks they can do on their own, let them get on with the job, and have them report to the group when they finish.

Another person to look out for is the one who has a different agenda to the rest of the group. This is the person who sees the group work primarily as an opportunity to gain promotion, or to prevent someone else from being promoted. When this happens we talk of that member having a secret agenda: that member has a different goal to the rest of the group and will usually harm the work of the group when it doesn't match his or her own goal.

GROUP BUILDING AND MAINTENANCE

During the conflict stage, members of the group are still trying to get on with one another. They will still be polite, careful not to say anything which could be misunderstood, and most importantly, they will still be looking for approval from other members of the group. By the time they are ready to move to the next stage they will know each other well enough to predict how each one will act under various circumstances. They will, by now, know who gets impatient, who needs extra information, who understands things easily, and so on. This knowledge helps the group to move away from the process of building the group to the business of dealing with its task.

RISKING ERROR

Most of us, in our daily lives, try very hard to avoid making mistakes because we find it embarrassing or humiliating. We don't want the people around us to know that we are not as good as we think they are. But if anything worthwhile is to be achieved, we have to take chances, and the biggest one has to be the chance that we may be wrong sometimes. On the other hand, we should never condemn anyone else's ideas without some thought. After all, the most outrageous idea may turn out to be the invention of the century.

We need to understand, though, that before we can take this risk, we have to trust all the members of the group. We will never risk making any errors until we are confident that no one will ridicule us.

HUMILITY

This is the ability to accept that we are not indispensable: that nothing will completely fail if we are not involved. Peter's problem is that he does believe that things can't go on without him. He thinks that no one else could be the leader, that the group absolutely needs him and that it will not function if he leaves. It's always a mistake to think like this: none of us is irreplaceable. We are all unique and each of us has a special combination of talents and skills, but there will always be someone else who can take our place. They may do things differently, but that doesn't make them better or worse, just different.

TRUST

Trust is the confidence of knowing that another person will not harm you. You have trust in another person when you believe that they will help you in a risky or difficult situation. Trust is closely related to self-esteem, which we discussed in chapter 2. If we feel good about ourselves we are more likely to feel good about others. When we feel good we are more likely to trust others. In part, this seems to be related to our feeling that we ourselves can be trusted. We only feel that way when our self-esteem is high.

So we can say that trust is having the confidence to believe that the other members of the group will behave in a way which is beneficial for each individual as well as for the group as a whole.

The communication between members is an important element in trust. When communication is open and honest, and when goals are clear and acceptable there is more likely to be trust than when these conditions don't exist.

A type of behaviour which we will come across at some time when we're part of a group is that of the bossy person—the authoritarian. This person usually doesn't trust anyone. Bossy people will delegate work and then keep interfering, convinced that no one else can do things as well as they can. They not only have no trust in others, but also never give others any grounds for trusting them. This is because we don't like to be controlled. When we feel that someone is trying to control us we become defensive and resist. The person who tries to control us is actually sending us unspoken messages that we are stupid, lazy or inadequate. None of us likes to be told anything like that, so we feel threatened and fight back.

On the other hand, when we are given respect, shown that we are capable and given credit for being intelligent, we respond by trusting the other person and being cooperative.

There is just one more point on this subject: trust is one of the behaviour patterns that is set up very early in our lives. People who have not had an early foundation of trust will find it difficult to give and accept trust in adulthood. This is not to say that they will never trust, just that it will take longer for them to build up an atmosphere of trust for themselves.

STRESS

How do you know when you are stressed? You could have any of a long list of symptoms: tiredness, irritation, mood swings and lethargy are just a few. When you have trouble getting to sleep at night, don't have much energy in the mornings, lose your appetite, lose your enthusiasm or lose your memory, you are probably suffering from stress. Even acne, colds, headaches and pains in the back and shoulders can be caused by stress. That's not to say that stress is always the cause of these symptoms, so, as they always tell you on television, if symptoms persist, see your doctor. But, before you do, why not try some relaxation and stress-reducing exercises on your own.

Everyone has their own way of responding to stress and everyone needs to work out their own way of coping with it. The best we can hope to do in a book like this is to look at some of the ways that other people deal with stress, and list some useful tips.

One of the simplest ways to deal with stress is to practise relaxation. This is not as difficult as you may imagine. A simple relaxation exercise which can be learnt during an unstressful time is this.

Sit in a comfortable chair with your feet on the floor and your hands lying in your lap. Close your eyes and concentrate on your breathing. When you are breathing evenly, count to five slowly. Then picture, in your mind's eye, a place you would like to be: it may be under a big umbrella on a sunny beach, it might be in a cosy room with an open fire, or on a grassy patch under some trees by a river. The important thing about it is that it's your private place. It doesn't have to exist anywhere except in your imagination, and you don't ever have to tell anyone about it. What you have to learn to do, when you close your eyes for a minute or two, is be able to take yourself to your 'place' to recharge your batteries. You do need to practise this a few times under non-stressful conditions before it will work, but once you have the knack it really can work wonders. Sometimes even just knowing that it's there can help. When the meeting gets stormy, or the work is piling up, or you just feel as though everything's getting on top of you, take a minute or two to visit your 'place' and you'll come back feeling much better.

Another good thing about doing this is that it slows the action down a bit, and can help other people to unwind too, even when they don't understand exactly what you are doing.

Of course, there are other ways of dealing with specific instances of stress. You could look at the problem which is causing the stress and try to find a solution to it. For example, something in the work practice in your area may cause you stress. It would be a good idea to talk the problem through with the other people involved in this practice and try to come to some mutually agreeable solution which would ease the stress on everyone.

But, remember, your stress is your problem and your health is your responsibility. Learning to cope with your own stress—to minimise it whenever possible—is something you can and should do as soon and as well as you possibly can.

HANDLING CONFLICT

Conflict can show up in many different ways: aggression, avoidance, or subversion, to name just a few. The best way to deal with conflict is to bring the problem into the open and have the people in conflict discuss the matter, preferably with a third person present. The aim of conflict resolution is to reach agreement and most often this will mean compromise. That doesn't mean that one of the people in the conflict will lose, but that they will negotiate until they reach agreement. Of course this will mean that each side will have to give a little. In the language of conflict resolution experts, what we are hoping to reach is a win–win situation. This way, no one will feel bad and no one will have the chance to stand on anyone's face. Other possibilities in conflict situations are win–lose, lose–win or lose–lose, none of which should need any explanation.

Our Western society operates on a social contract basis: we talk things through, we try to see the other person's point of view as well as our own, and we usually compromise so that both parties accept the solution to the conflict.

So, to deal with conflict we need negotiating skills. These are skills which we all learnt at a very early stage in our lives. When you were told, at the age of five or six, to go to bed and you asked for just one more story, or one more drink, or five minutes more, you were negotiating. Because what you were really saying was something like this: 'If you give me one more story (or drink, or five minutes), *then* I'll go to bed quietly'.

So, an easy way to explain what negotiation is all about is to use the model of '*If . . . then . . .*' If you give me this, then I'll give you that—where 'this' is something I want and 'that' is something you want. This form of negotiation is something we all practise almost everyday in order to live comfortably with the people around us. But because it is something we usually do instinctively, most of us haven't thought of it as one of our skills.

This happens a lot in group or team work: we have a lot of the skills we need but we don't realise that we have them. We have been using them—sometimes well and sometimes badly—in all our dealings within our family groups, in school with our fellow students and in our workplaces with our co-workers around us. What we need to do is examine our skills one by one and try to improve on those which aren't as good as they could be.

It may be less threatening to practise negotiating at home first. Think of something which members of the household all dislike doing and then something no one minds doing. Tell them you have to learn about negotiating skills for work. Ask them to cooperate in a practice session using a situation with which you're all familiar so that it will feel more real.

Get each member to state what they want. For example:

1st person: I don't mind cooking dinner but I hate cleaning up.
2nd person: I'd also rather cook than clean.
3rd person: I'd rather clean up after dinner. I'm not mad about cooking and I hate shopping.
4th person: I like shopping and I don't mind cooking or cleaning.
1st person: It looks easy—two of us take turns to cook and two take turns to clean.

2nd person:	What about the shopping then?
3rd person:	What about when I do feel like cooking? Who does the cleaning then?
1st person:	There's another problem: if two of us take turns then do we do alternate nights or alternate weeks? I mean, what happens when I have to work late or go straight to a meeting and it's my turn to cook?

As you can see, there is no simple solution even though it seemed there might be in the beginning. Later in this discussion the members of the household may decide to extend the negotiations to include such chores as mowing the lawn and putting out the garbage.

The point of the exercise, for you, is to have experienced the negotiation process among people you know and live with. It's important, though, to allow enough time for the process to be worked through to a solution with which everyone feels happy.

GROUP GOAL-SETTING

Although it will be difficult to achieve any significant goals during this second stage in the life of the group, it is important that long-term goals should be set. These may change during the next stage: they may be extended or expanded or they may even be reduced in order to be more realistic. Perhaps a goal that is set at this stage will seem later to be either too long-term or too ambitious. When this happens the group may become discouraged because it can't see the light at the end of the tunnel.

In this case, the group should break the larger goal down into manageable chunks of smaller, achievable goals which will bring a sense of accomplishment to those involved. This is important because each time a goal is achieved—a job finished—there is incentive to go on to the next task.

CASE STUDY

Wendy has been chosen as group secretary. She is responsible for organising future meetings. The group decides, at the end of each meeting, when the next one will take place, but Wendy has to arrange where it will be. She needs to find a room with enough seating for eight people, although extra chairs could be brought in. There is no spare room with enough space. The only places Wendy can think of are the staff training rooms and the canteen.

The training rooms are fully booked for the time she needs. That leaves the canteen. The group had decided that meetings should take place at eleven in the morning as that seemed to be a time that suited everyone. This would be a busy time in the canteen because some of the early shift people start arriving for lunch soon after eleven.

For the first meeting Wendy and Han Li find a space at the back of the despatch area. They have to bring in a table and some chairs and it isn't a good place to have a meeting. It's noisy and cold and everyone feels irritable. Nothing much is achieved and the meeting lasts about twenty minutes. They agree to make a permanent booking of a training room early in the morning, before the training staff begin using the room.

This is good for some people: Han Li starts work at 7.30 every day, others begin their shifts at 8 am and only Susie will have to come in earlier than her usual 9 am starting time.

Before we join the group for its fourth meeting we should look at what it's achieved so far.

- Margaret has been chosen as the group leader.
- The team has made a list of six items, in various parts of the factory and offices, which were observed to be dangerous.

After some heated discussion at the third meeting it was decided to work on the air-conditioning problem first, because it affected a lot of people and it seemed easy to fix.

For the fourth meeting, Peter has been asked to collect some information about the number of people in his section who are affected by the lack of air-conditioning. Maria had offered to find out from the maintenance staff what had been done in the past about getting the air-conditioning fixed. Xuan had promised to find out more about the air-conditioning system itself.

In this meeting people are still vying for power. Peter is still resentful of Margaret and thinks the others are stupid. He can't see the point of the exercise and is passively undermining things by not pulling his weight. Peter arrives at the meeting about ten minutes late. He walks in and sits down without saying anything, but makes quite a lot of noise with his chair and then with the papers and pens he puts on the table. Wendy, who is speaking when he comes in, stops and looks up. When Peter offers no explanation, she carries on reading the minutes of the previous meeting. As she gets to the end Peter says: 'All a waste of time, if you ask me, reading all that guff.' No one responds. There's a short pause before Margaret speaks.

Margaret: Peter, what information do you have for the group?
Peter: I haven't had time to look into any of this stuff yet. Too much real work in my section. Air-conditioning's not important.

Margaret would like to tell Peter that she wishes he would leave the group, but she doesn't quite have the courage. She knows she should assert her authority. The group did choose her as the leader, but she finds Peter intimidating. She makes a note to speak to Steve about this problem later.

Meanwhile, Susie is the one who gets angry.

Susie: This is supposed to be real work, too, you know. And if you don't want to be here why don't you just drop out?
Peter: I'm here because I'm the most senior person on this committee. How can I just drop out?
Susie: Well, I thought we were all equal in this group.

Peter leans back in his chair and looks slowly round the group.

Peter: (Sneering) Does it look like we're all equal?

Indira takes exception to this. She stands up.

Indira: I do not want to be here with you any more.

Han Li and Xuan look at one another uncertainly and then also stand up to leave.

Wendy: I agree with them. And Susie's right—we are supposed to be all equal here.

All this gives Margaret some courage.

Margaret: I think it would be better if you left the group, Peter.

The assertiveness we talked about in chapter 2 is coming into use here. Margaret needed some support from the other members of the group to be able to deal with Peter. One of the benefits of this incident is that it will strengthen the unity of the group. They now realise that they form a group and that they will all be considered equal, though there will still be some friction. It would be unrealistic to expect not to have any arguments or disagreements in a group, even when members have been working together for some time and know each other quite well.

It would have taken a lot of courage on Indira's part to walk out of the meeting. Her knowledge of English is good enough for her to understand what Peter is saying, whereas Xuan and Han Li mainly understand the tone of voice and the body language Peter uses. We have to remember that because we feel superior doesn't necessarily make the other person feel inferior—it just makes them feel insulted! So we get back to all the things we have said about tolerance, acceptance, assertiveness and good communication skills.

In this section we have dealt with many issues, all related to the growth of the group as a whole. The group members managed to get rid of Peter by acting together, by not accepting his judgement of them. This would probably give them a stronger group identity. Having achieved this small victory, they will feel more confident about the tasks ahead of them. Margaret may feel that she should have done more to stand up for the group against Peter and she may feel the need to assert her authority in other small ways. The group has shown, though, that it could deal with a problem. The members have given one another moral support in a situation where they felt they were being looked down on and dealt successfully with a person who tried to intimidate them.

Indira speaks English with a fairly strong accent. In her own country she held a fairly senior position; she is used to being in charge of people even though she hasn't yet achieved this status in her job here. She is not afraid of people like Peter and has the communication skills to understand his feeling of superiority and his chauvinism. Her treatment of Peter in the meeting is assertive: she states her position without passing judgement on anyone else's behaviour. She doesn't leave the subject open to any discussion.

Han Li speaks barely enough English to get by. He is trying to improve his language skills as well as his job prospects. He is considerably older than he looks and is worried about keeping his job. In the way of his Asian culture he smiles a lot and seems to say yes, even when he has not fully understood what he has been told. This could cause the group some problems, but he will make up for these by working very hard when he does understand what needs to be done.

Maria also has some difficulties with her English, but mainly with reading and writing. She didn't have much schooling in her own country and has always had the kind of job she has here: doing unskilled work in a factory. She is determined to make the most of the opportunity of working with the group and her enthusiasm is an asset.

GROWING—REACHING COHESION

Before the group can progress to the next stage, it has to resolve some issues. The main one is the allocation and establishment of roles so that all members know exactly what is expected of them. Each person must feel comfortable with the others and each must feel secure and accepted by the group.

There must also be an understanding of the process of the difference between the things which must be done to maintain the group and the things that must be done to complete the task. Sometimes these overlap and it is difficult to see where one starts and the other ends. For example, making a cup of tea and listening sympathetically to a group member who is having a problem finding the information they need is obviously a part of group maintenance. Helping that member to find the information, even when it cuts into other members' time, is both maintenance and task-oriented.

This brings us to another skill we will need to develop a little more at each stage of group life—listening. As the group grows and develops we need to sharpen our listening skills. We need to begin to listen on another level and start to notice subtle signals like a lift of the eyebrow, a frown, a wave of the hand. These add to the meaning of the words we use and noticing them is part of that good listening which takes place between people who have empathy—the ability to tune in to each other's feelings.

Another important development at this stage is that members of the group will be able to trust each other. With this trust comes the ability to risk being wrong. This sounds strange: after all we probably risk being wrong almost every time we say anything. But when we think about it a little more seriously, it really isn't silly. We often choose not to say what we think if we believe that somebody else in the group may find it wrong or ridiculous. In the same way, we sometimes wonder why someone said something which we feel is wrong or stupid. We need to reach a point where we can feel safe in saying things and knowing that other members of the group will accept them, examine them and discuss them before throwing them out.

One other characteristic we need to work on before we go on to the next stage is humility—the ability to realise that we are part of the group, not the whole or even the most important part. We need to understand that the group will function just as well without us, that someone else could easily take our place without causing the world—or the group—to collapse. This notion of the group collapsing brings us to another possibility: that someone may actually want this to happen.

SABOTAGE AND SUBVERSION

These two activities, both of which are designed to undermine the group, usually go unnoticed in the early stages. Anyone who becomes subversive does so without airing their problems. The subversive person is one who hides feelings of resentment. They will feel that they have been insulted, ridiculed or put down in some way, but won't be able to discuss it openly with anyone. The feeling builds up and they begin to undermine the work of the group. Worse than that, at this stage, is the damage they can do to the group process.

For example, Jack feels that he should have been the leader of his sports club but instead that role went to Fred, who is more popular but has not been with the club for as long as Jack. As the head of the committee, Fred would like to raise money to build a new clubhouse. Everyone thinks this is a great idea, even Jack. But Jack resents Fred getting the credit for it.

To begin with, Jack questions every suggestion put forward by Fred. Not only does this take up a lot of time at the meetings, it makes some people begin to doubt that Fred is really the wonderboy they all thought he was. As long as Jack asks the questions in a friendly, non-aggressive tone and sounds as though he means well, nobody will think of this as an attack.

When this has been going on for a while, Jack makes a mental note of who is beginning to doubt Fred. He then talks to them individually, perhaps over a drink, telling them about 'poor Fred' having problems at work. Or perhaps Jack hints that Fred's problems are at home with his family. Nothing specific is said—Jack just suggests that the pressure of all this may be a bit much and that Fred just can't cope. Another time Jack might talk to one or two people before the meeting and suggest that no pressure be put on Fred tonight—'he's got problems, you know'. If we all just go along with things the meeting could finish early and give poor Fred a break, says Jack. All this makes Jack look like a nice guy, caring about Fred, worrying about Fred's problems, but carefully undermining him all the same.

Sabotage is slightly different—it's a deliberate jamming up of the group's workings. It can be done by feeding in false information, by leaving out important information or steps in a process, or doing things in the wrong order. There are as many ways of performing sabotage as there are people who want to do it. The worst thing about it is that it doesn't show up until it has happened. Sometimes it is difficult to find the saboteur, but if the damage is to be repaired the culprit must be found. No one else will know what harm has been caused.

4

COHESION

DURING THIS STAGE, members of the group become concerned with mutual affection, acceptance by other members, willingness to share information and the desire to build a team spirit. There is also a more open-minded attitude within the group and listening skills usually improve noticeably in this stage.

This is also the time when the task work begins to speed up somewhat as members are more willing to share information, work together for the good of the group and even, perhaps, change their attitudes or behaviour to arrive at a win–win situation. Members are learning to work together because they should, by now, know each other reasonably well, and there should be a substantial element of trust and acceptance.

In some groups, especially those whose members have contact with each other outside the group, this stage may be reached very quickly. Other groups may take longer.

On a personal and interpersonal level we need to think about these topics: trust and acceptance, affection, open-mindedness, cohesion and the building of team spirit.

ACCEPTANCE

By the cohesion stage, the group members should all accept each other and respect each other's opinions. This is vital if there is to be contribution from everyone. As long as any member feels that they are not part of the group, they will be reluctant to put forward any ideas. In earlier stages there will have been a very real fear that ideas may not be accepted; that they would be ridiculed or laughed at, especially when the group was looking for solutions to problems.

As you will see in the following section on decision making and problem solving, it is important to build and maintain a good level of trust between members if activities like brainstorming and finding new and interesting solutions are to succeed. We are not willing to share creative, innovative ideas with people who, we feel, do not accept us. As long as we feel that we are not accepted our main fear is that we will be criticised and none of us willingly exposes ourselves to that.

So, the more trust and acceptance there is among members of the group, the less inhibited everyone will feel. And once inhibitions are lowered, creative ideas will flow more easily, people will be willing to share more daring ideas and some good solutions will come out. Evaluating those ideas is another matter. The main thing is for everyone to feel that they can voice their opinions and ideas freely and without criticism.

TEAM SPIRIT

By the time the group reaches this stage there should be a good team spirit. All the members of the group should know each other well enough for trust, affection and a willingness to work together to be apparent. There should also be enough loyalty within the group to withstand a reasonable amount of criticism from outside.

You will find, at this stage, that if a member of the team betrays the trust of the others, the group will punish that person by ignoring them, freezing them out or chastising them quite severely. The betrayal could be something quite simple, like giving information to outsiders about group activities or even group behaviour. Or it could be more serious. In any case, the 'punishment' the group imposes is often quite out of proportion to the perceived 'offence', but will be directly related to the level of unity in the group. If there is a strong sense of belonging among the group members then the betrayal will seem much worse than at earlier stages in the life of the team, when bonding has not yet taken place.

DECISION MAKING AND PROBLEM SOLVING

There are several ways of solving problems and a group, especially a small group of people who trust one another, should have no trouble coming up with a range of solutions when necessary. We could use brainstorming, or mindmaps or information gathering or surveys, or we could just try the first solution that comes to mind. Possibly, your group will come up with too many solutions, or perhaps everyone will wait for someone else to think of a solution and there won't be any. This is why a brainstorming session is a good idea.

If you've never taken part in a brainstorming here's how it works. The idea is to get everyone to put in their suggestions. That sentence bears repeating: we want to get *everyone* to put in their suggestions. That's why trust is so important. People will only contribute ideas when they feel safe from criticism and ridicule. Once we understand this we can set up the following ground rules:

1 There must be no criticism of ideas.
2 Wild ideas are expected and accepted.
3 The quantity of ideas counts, not the quality.
4 Build on the ideas of other group members where possible.
5 Focus on a single simple problem, not a complicated one.
6 Be relaxed.
7 Make sure all members' ideas are heard.
8 Record all ideas.
9 Minimum time for a session should be fifteen minutes.

The reason for this last rule will become obvious the first time you take part in a session. At first, everyone has lots of ideas—all fairly obvious and ordinary—then there will be a gap. This may last anything from a few seconds to a full minute. When this happens an inexperienced facilitator is likely to give up. Most of us feel uncomfortable with silence which goes on for too long but in this case it is worth waiting because eventually more ideas will surface. The trouble seems to be that we are all lazy thinkers. We need quite a bit of pushing to really try that little bit harder to think of something new or different or crazy. It also takes practice.

Making that effort leads to the next stage, where the ideas become crazier, more innovative and maybe even impossible. This is the time when really interesting ideas appear, as long as the atmosphere remains one of trust and affection. The main thing at this stage is to keep a record of all the ideas which the group has come up with: evaluation comes later.

Now let's turn to decision making: this is a topic about which there are shelves full of books; books that tell us how to make decisions, why it's difficult to make decisions, how many ways there are of making decisions. What we will look at in this short section is the relationship between decision making and groups. Further on in this chapter you will find the heading 'Groupthink and the risky shift' where we will look at some of the pitfalls of the decision-making process.

Now we will look at some good ways that a group can reach a decision and what happens when it really is a group decision.

First, let's look at how we might reach our decision. In some ways this depends on how the group arrived at the list of possible solutions or actions on which the decision needs to be based. For example, if you had a brainstorming session, there will be a lot of ideas from which to choose. Discussion by all the members of the group will probably be a good way to reduce the number of possibilities.

When there are only a few possibilities, whether as a result of discussion after brainstorming or because there was just a short list to begin with, the group could list the factors which would influence the decision. They may need to take into account such things as the cost in dollars and cents of implementing the decision; the number of people needed; the time it would take; how much outside help would be required and so on. These factors could then be put into order of importance.

Perhaps the job needs to be done within a week. The group would then need to base its decision on factors like the availablity of the experts needed for the job, the cost of getting work done in a hurry, and the possibility of an extension of time for completion of the task. And so, by a process of evaluation and elimination, a decision can be reached.

The important point here is that it is vital that the group be in total agreement about the decision. If this is not the case, then the decision will not be acceptable. Only when every member of the group feels happy with the decision will there be cooperation and cohesion in the task work.

Perhaps, reading this, you feel that it may take forever for your group to reach agreement on the course of action to be taken. Usually, this means that there are members who are not committed to the decision and their reasons for disagreement should be looked at. By acknowledging that we have different points of view, different standards, different fears and hopes and dreams, and examining these carefully, we do two things: we help people to overcome their fears and reservations, and we look more carefully at the decisions we are making. Having to explain your ideas and justify them makes you look at them more carefully, makes you think about them more deeply and analyse them, and the possible outcomes, more closely.

Once the group is in complete agreement, everything will go along much more smoothly. The reason for this is that when we feel we have contributed positively to the decision-making process, we feel committed to making the solution work. Take these two scenes as examples.

Mr Blunder: The factory will be moving to the new place on Wednesday. I want everything packed by Tuesday afternoon. Any problems, I'll be in my office.

Everyone goes back to their usual work, muttering, and no one does any packing or preparing until Mr Blunder comes back to supervise this on Tuesday. On the other hand, in another department, we find this scene.

Mr Fern: I asked you all to come in here to talk about the move next Wednesday. Everything has to be ready for the removalists by Tuesday afternoon. What do you need

	and how will we fit this into the work we all have anyway?
Wayne:	Boxes and some of that foam packing stuff.
Gloria:	We could start packing things as we use them. You know, when we finish with something and don't think we'll need it again before the move.
Monty:	If we don't finish will we have to work overtime?
Mr Fern:	Probably, but I'd rather we didn't.
Monty:	I don't want to work overtime. Maybe I can do only urgent work today and then do some packing.
Wayne:	Yeah, and I can do the same tomorrow. And if that's not enough then we could do it again on Monday.

You probably won't have any difficulty working out which department had fewer problems with the move.

Decision making is not really an easy process and some people get so nervous about it that they avoid it whenever they can. They end up letting other people make decisions for them and just let things happen. When you learn to make decisions you take charge of your own life: you plan where you're going.

NEGOTIATION STRATEGIES AND STYLES

Most of us learn some form of negotiation quite early in our lives, We learn to bargain for things we want and can't get for ourselves. In families which operate on a cooperative basis, where everyone is responsible for their share of the chores, there will often be bargaining.

Brian:	I have to go to a meeting tomorrow evening and it's my turn to wash the dishes. Would you do them for me, Neill?
Neill:	Sure, if you do my laundry on Saturday.
Brian:	That's impossible. I've got footy practice on Saturday. Can't I just wash the dishes for you sometime when it's your turn?
Neill:	No. We tried that once before and you never paid your debt. I want to know now what you'll do in exchange. And I want to know when you'll do it.

56

Brian: OK, OK, how about I mow the lawn on Friday.
                That's your job this week, isn't it?
Neill: Right, but don't you forget or this will be the last
                time we do this kind of trade. Next time you can just
                pay me money to do your chores.

If you have to negotiate outside your family, you would have to
be more serious and better organised than Brian and Neill. There are
four steps to good negotiating and once you learn to use them you
will become a much better negotiator. Being a good negotiator makes
you a good communicator too, and you'll find that you will get along
much better with people.

These are the four steps to good negotiating.

1 Preparation

This consists of thinking about what you want and how you are
prepared to get it. You need to think about the point of view of the
other person as well as your own needs.

It makes sense to write things down at this stage. On one side of
the page, list what you would really like: everything you would like
to get. On the other side, list the minimum you will settle for. Now
take another sheet of paper and list the things you have to offer the
other person in exchange for the things you want. Would they be
happy with what you are offering? Would you, if the positions were
reversed? Think carefully about the value of what you are offering—
not the value to you but the value to the other person. Good
negotiation is about offering things which are easy for you to give,
but valuable to the other person. You can be sure that the other
person will know that the things you are asking for will have high
value to you. That doesn't necessarily mean that they are of high
value to them, but it does give them the advantage to know that you
value something.

2 Discussion

This is the beginning of the face-to-face process. Each side will make
an offer, and it's important to ensure that these offers are realistic.
Then, you will withdraw a little. There may be some small talk at

this point as each side thinks about what has been offered. Then there will be signalling. This is recognised by words like 'yes, you can have . . .', and 'but I want . . .'

After this initial statement of positions and some signalling, the process moves to the next stage.

3 Proposing

Tentative offers which move from the opening position are made. Expressions like 'what if . . . then perhaps . . .' indicate that you are both prepared to move.

At this stage you need to be prepared to move from your opening position. But remember, don't move too far or too fast. Leave yourself something to bargain with. Use the list you made in the first stage, while you were thinking things through calmly. You wrote down all the things you want, and then you wrote down the least you would accept. Don't go straight from the top to the bottom. Compromise is what you are looking for, and it should come somewhere that looks like halfway between what you see as ideal and what the other person sees that way.

4 Bargaining

This is really an extension of the last step. Negotiation, as we have already seen, is a process of give and take, so make sure that you are not doing all the giving. For everything you give you should get something in return.

Towards the end of this last phase make sure that both sides agree on what has been agreed on. The signalling in the second phase indicated to the other side that you were prepared to move. The bargaining at the end is to get what you want while keeping the other side happy with what they are getting.

If you go into a negotiation without being willing to give anything and the other side is also not willing to give, then there will be no result. When one side is willing to give but the other isn't, there will be bad feelings afterwards: the side that gave will feel cheated. Only when both sides are willing to give or to move from their opening positions will there be mutual satisfaction. In negotiation jargon this is called a win–win outcome.

Having read this you may be wondering: what if they're more powerful than me? When you're in this situation, remember to be assertive, do your preparation and keep your cool. Don't let the other side harass you. If you really want what you are going for and you feel you have the right to ask for it, then be calm and firm and take your notes into the meeting with you so you can look at them when you need to.

What if they won't play? In this case I don't think there is much you can do. You can state your request, make some reasonable offer and then leave. Occasionally you may find that the other person is nervous about the negotiation process or afraid of people who sound too assertive. They may have had previous experiences where they came out of a negotiation feeling that the other side had bulldozed them into accepting less than they wanted. This could have left them angry and afraid of the process. If you give them time to think about the offer you have made they may come back to you later and make an offer of their own. If this happens you could take the timing for your next move from them: nice and slow so you don't frighten them off, giving them enough time to think about things.

In the end, what you want is a win–win situation: one where both sides are happy with the outcome.

NORMS

This word, which simply means accepted standards, can cover quite a few areas: we speak of norms of behaviour, dress, attitude and beliefs, and what we mean is that people have the same standards of dress or behaviour and so on as we have. When we don't have the same standards as a group we would like to become part of, we have little trouble changing. For example, if you want to be accepted as a Mason you buy yourself a dinner suit. If you join the Guides or the Scouts you wear a uniform and behave according to their standards.

Norms regarding clothing, food and behaviour can be very rigid. The desire for acceptance is so great in most of us that we will do almost anything that is asked of us by a group we wish to join. We will do things in a group which we would never dream of doing as individuals. As long as the group is satisfying some need in us this will be true. This is why people will subject themselves to the bizarre and horrific initiation practices we occasionally hear about. We are, after all, social animals.

Remember James from chapter 1? During the week he conforms to all the norms of the stockbroking world in which he operates. On weekends he operates according to a completely different set of norms: his way of speaking is different, so is his behaviour, his clothing and even his attitude. This is the wonderful thing about human beings: we can, and often do, change for a wide variety of reasons. The basic ingredient to make change take place is motivation: a desire to change. No other person can make you change. They might influence your behaviour under certain circumstances and for a short period, but real, lasting change has to come from inside yourself. You are the only person who can change you.

Norms are important because they allow individuals to predict, with a certain amount of accuracy, the sort of behaviour they can expect from other members of the group. They also create a sense of unity and as the group goes about building a team spirit it becomes increasingly important for all members to behave in the same way, or dress in the same way, or use the same slang or jargon. Our friend James knows that if he uses the jargon of the stock exchange with his bikie mates, they will be surprised, confused and irritated. If he persists, the group will eventually freeze him out.

By the same token, if he went to work on Monday in his leather gear and boots he would not be very welcome at the stock exchange, no matter how good he may be at his job. So, you can see that group norms are very important for group membership and group unity.

There is an exception—called deviation—to these rules, and it will be discussed in chapter 5.

INITIATIVE

The ability to get things started is one of the greatest assets a group member can have. There will often be times when things slow down and almost come to a halt, and there will be other times when they don't even seem to get started. Usually, there will be at least one initiator in every group. This will be someone who has the ability to see what needs to be done and is then able to motivate other members to get going.

One skill that the initiator usually has is the ability to break large tasks into manageable chunks. You could think of these smaller chunks as bite-size. And of course you shouldn't ever bite off more than you can chew! Being able to do this makes the larger task seem less threatening, less overwhelming.

VALUES, BELIEFS AND ATTITUDES

Our values are our ideas about what's good or bad, our beliefs indicate our acceptance of what is true or false and our attitudes are the way we respond to things, how we behave. Our values, beliefs and attitudes are formed in our earliest years and, even though they may change as we grow older, we usually hang on to them quite firmly.

Our values grow out of basic human needs and the world we live in. This means that our environment, our society and our culture help determine what we will accept as good or reject as bad. One culture may value accumulation of material possessions while another values sharing and cooperation more highly. In the former, stealing would be an offence and cooperation a surprising and unusual activity. In the latter, stealing would be a strange idea and competitiveness would be surprising.

Belief refers to our sense of truth and falsehood. We know that sometimes it is difficult to determine the truth: some things are absolutely true or absolutely false but some are in between—probably true or probably false and some things we just don't know. It is important to remember that our beliefs are usually things we want to believe, even when someone shows us that they are not logical. We develop our system of beliefs from our own experiences, from the beliefs of people we consider 'authorities' and from the response we get from other people around us.

Attitude is the way we feel about things and how we behave in response to them. We could have a positive or a negative attitude towards things depending on whether we feel attracted to them or not. Attitudes are a bit like values because they express our feelings about good and bad. The difference is that attitudes are more easily changed than values.

There are two aspects of attitude we need to examine: the intensity of the attitude and the relative importance of the issue. For example, you may have a very strong like or dislike of a certain kind of vegetable, but vegetables are not a terribly important issue for most of us. However, you may not care about your health even though this is an important issue.

The most important lesson we need to learn regarding values and beliefs is that ours may be very different to other people's but that doesn't make any of us right or wrong. Our attitude towards other people's values and beliefs will be totally different to our attitude to our own values and beliefs. That isn't hard to understand. What we need to learn is to respect each other's values and beliefs and develop positive attitudes towards all of them.

We also need to remember that our values, beliefs and attitudes have been learned and can, therefore, be unlearned or relearned or replaced by other values, beliefs or attitudes. Changing any or all of these will affect our behaviour. When I have a positive attitude towards you and your beliefs, I will respect you and behave in a more friendly way. This, in the long run, will also make me feel better about myself because we all want to be liked and when I like you and show that I do, then there is more chance that you will like me too.

COOPERATION

I'm sure you will agree that this is the most important concept in the whole team process. Cooperation needs trust, affection and honesty; it needs a supportive atmosphere and it needs a positive attitude; it needs acceptance and a willingness to change. But most of all it needs team spirit.

A group containing a member who is too independent or too competitive will endure constant feelings of friction between this person and the others. Most of the members will have a feeling of group unity, with this member on the outside. The outsider is likely to want personal recognition for activities which the others feel should be part of the group effort.

In one group the competitive behaviour of one member was felt right from the beginning. At first the other members thought it was just a matter of time to get Wayne to join in the group effort. Perhaps he's just shy, said Sally. He hasn't done this sort of thing before, said Fay. I think he's just not interested in being part of our group, was Don's opinion. By the time the first group task was almost complete, Wayne still hadn't made the effort to do any of the things the rest of the group felt were necessary. He hadn't put in any of the information he had collected, he didn't come to planning sessions and he communicated with the others mainly in writing.

The group Wayne belonged to worked on several tasks during its two-year life. The first task was a small one: to present a body of information to a large group within which the smaller one operated. Each member of the small group would verbally present some part of the information, using overhead transparencies and photocopied handouts.

All the information had been collected by members and then pooled. Everyone cooperated except Wayne. He collected the information he had been asked to find, but refused to put it in the communal pool. It was his and he would present it. He even printed his own handouts, with his name as author, for distribution at the presentation.

By this time the other members of the group were beginning to feel that they had a problem on their hands. If the group was going to function effectively for two years, and if it was to perform well, then something had to be done about Wayne.

There are several options at this stage: the group could find out what Wayne's reason is for not cooperating; it could freeze him out; it could put the case for his exclusion to him and see how he reacts; it could call in an independent adviser; it could have a meeting with the adviser and then let the adviser meet separately with Wayne.

In the end it turned out that Wayne had felt that he had been given more than his fair share of work at the beginning. When he had pointed this out, no one appeared to hear him. Perhaps he was not forceful enough at that stage. So he went off and did what he had been asked to do, but no longer felt as if he belonged or even wanted to belong to the group. After several talks, initially between the adviser and Wayne, then between the adviser and other group members, and finally everyone together, it was agreed that Wayne would be helped to become more assertive.

OPEN-MINDEDNESS

Sometimes, our beliefs and experiences stop us from listening to others with an open mind. Quite often we aren't even aware of what causes these prejudices. It may be something as simple as a bad experience we once had. We may even have forgotten the actual event, but the feeling it caused stays with us and surfaces under similar circumstances in the present. This is especially true if the experience happened early in your life and was a bad one.

Perhaps in your childhood you had an unpleasant experience involving a man with a scar on his face. As the memory of the incident fades you will forget the man's appearance. By the time you are an adult you may not consciously remember that he had a scar. You may, however, feel uneasy and distrustful of any man with any sort of scar on his face without really being able to explain why this is so.

As an adult I met a woman called Anthea, a fairly unusual and quite attractive name, but for no apparent reason I disliked her from the minute we were introduced. Several months later, Anthea's name came up in the course of a conversation in the presence of my mother. When she heard that I disliked this woman without any reason, she reminded me of an incident which happened when I was six years old involving a girl called Anthea. It had been the only physical fight I had ever had and it had clearly left a memory associated with the name.

Open-mindedness is not the easiest thing to achieve, but it is worth the effort. It means that we will get much more out of our interactions with other people. We will listen more carefully, understand better what is being said and give unbiased responses. In terms of better communication it pays to be open-minded.

Remember: a closed mind usually means closed ears too.

LISTENING

We learned quite a bit about listening in chaper 1 but because it is such an important skill we will look at some other aspects of it here.

Listening is not a passive activity. Real listening needs active involvement. It isn't only when you are speaking that your brain needs to be engaged. You also need to switch on your brain to listen properly. Good listening means learning to separate the facts from the opinions.

This can be as simple as understanding the difference between 'She's a lovely person and she types very well', and 'She's well groomed and her typing is good'. 'She's a lovely person' is an opinion; that her typing is good and that she is well groomed are facts which can be checked. There is little point in letting someone else's opinions upset us: they are, after all, entitled to hold those opinions, just as you are entitled to yours. It takes some practice not to become upset by others' opinions, but it's worth the effort.

Concentrate on what is being said, as well as the way it is being said. Don't let yourself be distracted by such things as the speaker's appearance, whether it is good or bad, or by strange mannerisms or speech peculiarities.

Let the words sink in before you respond. It's better not to answer in the heat of the moment because you may say something you could regret later. Allowing a few seconds silence at the end of someone else's speech shows that you are considering your reply carefully. And giving feedback, to show that you have understood, gives you time to think again about what has been said. Your response will then be better thought out, and quite probably better expressed.

Listeners and speakers should both remember that they are engaged in a two-way process, not a solitary activity. It may be useful to remember this.

| Tune in | Inquire | Listen | Evaluate |

Tune in: Be ready to listen from the beginning.

Inquire: Think of questions you either need to ask or look for

	answers to during the talk. Sometimes you can ask questions during the talk, other times you may need to wait until the speaker has finished.
Listen:	Here we mean listen actively. Be aware of other levels of communication such as the non-verbal signals, the tone of voice, the rate of speaking, the facial expressions of the speaker and so on.
Evaluate:	Make a preliminary decision, as the person is speaking, about whether you agree with what's being said. This will help you to listen more carefully.

When the listening takes place in a meeting, it is often helpful to take brief notes while others are speaking. Just write down key words or short phrases to remind yourself of the points made by others.

AFFECTION

As we get to know people better we develop a positive feeling toward them. This doesn't mean that they become intimate friends, but that we begin to feel that we know them, and will support them and cooperate with them in team activities.

Affection is identified by psychologists as one of the basic interpersonal needs. Trust and affection are both two-way streets. When you give trust and affection you will receive them in return, and one way of building these feelings is by a process called self-disclosure. It works a bit like this:

| Thelma: | Did you watch *Oliver* on the telly last night? |
| Alex: | Yes, wasn't it great? I've seen it about six times, now. |

Thelma and Alex have now discovered a little about one another. It may seem relatively unimportant, but they feel that they know one another just that bit better and, on another occasion, this will lead to further sharing of information about themselves. The more you find in common with another person the more likely it is that a friendship will develop.

TRUST

One of the most important factors that influences the successful interaction in a group is trust. It works two ways: we need to trust other members of the group and we need to feel that they trust us. We build trust by being reliable, dependable and cooperative. We show our trust in others by letting them get on with the things they have committed themselves to, by believing them when they give reasons for not having done things and by cooperating with them when they ask for help—and sometimes even before they ask for it.

In most groups someone will take the role of the 'trust builder'. This will be someone who accepts and supports the openness of other members of the group, who supports risk-taking on the part of individuals and encourages individuality. This person will also be good at smoothing ruffled feathers. They will be able to sense when the situation is becoming difficult. Quite often the 'trust builder' is also the 'people person' we spoke of in chapter 2 when we were discussing leadership. Being a good people person, the trust builder will know when to help and when to leave others alone. They will be able to keep up the enthusiasm and energy levels of the group.

When we trust the other people in our group we are more likely to be ourselves, to behave naturally. As long as we are unsure of other people we hide behind a stiff, formal role. We behave the way we think other people expect us to. We are often overly polite, we keep our real feelings hidden and are reluctant to voice our opinions because we are afraid of being ridiculed.

Once trust has been established, everyone begins to relax. At this stage, members of the group will be willing to relax and be more honest about the way they feel. They will share jokes, get passionate about things they believe in, and even show when they are angry.

By the time the group gets to this stage—the stage we have called cohesion—there should be a large measure of trust between members. If there isn't, then this stage is not going as it should, and the group may complete its task, but it will be with difficulty. There will certainly not be any feeling of unity or cooperation.

In families there can be a breakdown of trust if someone believes that their problems are being discussed with outsiders by other members of the household, or when parents don't allow children to grow up. Many parents find it difficult to realise that their children have become adults with views and opinions of their own.

WILLINGNESS TO CHANGE

Change is inevitable. Once we accept this we may be able to accept changes in our lives a little more easily. Most of the things in our lives change quite slowly, but every so often something comes along which needs a faster change. It could be a new way of doing a job, it may be a new person in our lives or it may be the loss of someone or something. When change happens slowly we accept it more readily: we only have to alter small patterns of behaviour.

It's important to remember that change is a process of growth, even when we appear to have lost something. Whatever happens in our lives we will never be able to return to the way we were even yesterday. Bearing that in mind let's examine the process.

One important thing to remember is that we can only change our own behaviour. When we do, others may change their behaviour in response to us. So what you have to do is something like this. First, decide what to change, then try the new way. Think about it, try it again, check the result, perhaps make some more adjustments, try again and check the results once more. As you can see, it becomes repetitive. But life is a bit like that. We have to keep trying to get it right, don't we?

CONFORMITY

Almost two thousand years ago a Roman called Marcus Aurelius said, 'I often marvel that while each man loves himself more than anyone else, he sets less value on his own estimate than on the opinions of others'. To get a favourable opinion from other people, we do our best to conform. Even when we feel confident that our belief or opinion is correct, we will be swayed by those whose opinions we value. Experiments have shown that group pressure can cause people to say exactly the opposite of what they believe to be true. It is always easy to follow the majority, mainly because we all want so desperately to be accepted.

Conforming behaviour may become dangerous if we take on socially unacceptable beliefs or behaviour patterns in order to become members of a group. For example, teenagers will wear unusual clothes, or behave in unusual ways in order to conform to the gang, but when the gang or group expects them to behave in ways which they find morally wrong, they begin to feel torn between what they have always believed and what the gang is expecting them to do.

Even in fairly straightforward situations when we feel that we know right from wrong, we experience severe stress when events do not match our system of beliefs. When someone at work is cheating the system and everyone else is turning a blind eye, you may become extremely stressed if you feel that you may be dragged in too. At some time or another we all have to choose between conformity and our conscience. My advice is to go with your conscience: you have to live with yourself for a long time.

GROUPTHINK AND THE RISKY SHIFT

These are two interesting things which happen in groups. One—groupthink—is usually bad; the other—the risky shift—can be good or bad. They occur when a group is trying to solve a problem and make a decision.

Groupthink happens in two situations: when the group has a very strong and persuasive leader and a short time in which to finish a task; and when members of the group feel that the decision they make must please people outside the group.

One of the classic cases of groupthink was the decision to launch the Challenger space shuttle in January 1986. Engineers were convinced that conditions for the launch were unfavourable; that if the launch took place at the scheduled time they would not be responsible for the consequences. But the group responsible for the final decision felt that there was pressure on it not to delay the launch again. It had already been delayed several times and another delay would upset many people and disrupt schedules. So the launch went ahead with appalling results, and the truth only came out in the ensuing enquiry.

There are many other examples of groupthink throughout history, and it's easy to see how it can happen when we start thinking about what goes on in groups. We want to belong, we don't want to rock the boat. Everyone else seems so sure of themselves and of the decision that you begin to doubt yourself. You think, I must be missing something. Maybe I'm just dumb. If I say anything they'll think I'm stupid. So you go along with the majority.

It would be easy for me to say 'Don't worry about seeming silly, just ask for more information'. But I realise it's not like that in real life. We have to live not only with the decisions we make, but with the other people in the group and we want them to like us.

The risky shift occurs when, because we are part of a group, we no longer see ourselves as being individually responsible for any decisions the group makes. When this happens, the group may make decisions which no person in the group would make on their own. These decisions may carry the risk of harming people or institutions. Each one of us would be reluctant to set up a situation where there is any possibility that people could get hurt, but as a group we may be willing to take this chance. The reason seems to be similar to that given by people who, during wartime, do terrible things to the enemy because they can later claim that they were merely following orders: they argue that they were not really responsible for making the decision to do the deed.

EFFECTIVENESS

To a large degree, effectiveness depends on the way tasks are allocated. For example, some jobs are better done by one person. It's easy to see that we don't need a committee to order the office stationery. This is also true for any job that is repetitive or mechanical. Imagine a group of people operating a sewing machine.

On the other hand, complex tasks needing creative solutions are better tackled by a group. Of course, one bright, creative person may be better than a group of average individuals, but because we don't always have a bright, creative person handy, a group is a good alternative. Aristotle, an ancient Greek, pointed out that the whole is greater than the sum of the parts. Or, if you prefer something a bit more modern: two heads are better than one.

Effectiveness also depends on planning and delegating. In case you haven't learnt what delegating means, it's getting other people to help with the work—like this:

Joe: Will you please see that all these brochures are put into envelopes, addressed, stamped and posted by tonight, Jane.

Jane: Shane, will you please arrange a space in the back of the store with a table and four chairs. Karen, could you fetch all the brochures from Joe's office, please. Penny, please will you bring two boxes of envelopes down here. When you have all done those things we will all work on putting the brochures in the envelopes.

As you see, Jane understands delegating. In order to do it successfully, you need to have good communication skills. You need to gain cooperation from those to whom you delegate work. You need to follow through, in a calm, friendly way, to make sure that people have done the jobs you have given them and that they have done them satisfactorily.

One way to ensure that people will do things the way you want is to explain carefully what is to be done, then ask for feedback to check that they have understood you correctly. Right at the start, state clearly the standard you expect.

Paul: (Giving the cleaner a bucket and mop) This floor should be clean but not polished. If you polish the floor, people may slip and fall. Just mop it down and let it dry.

Phung: Floor not look good with no polish.

Paul: That's OK. Polish makes it dangerous. Do you understand 'dangerous'?

Phung: Yes, I understand. OK, no polish.

Delegating work also helps with planning. When there are several complex tasks waiting to be done, it is quicker to get people each to do some part and then bring everything together. This means some things can be done in a shorter time and resources can be used more efficiently.

GROWING TO CONSTRUCTION

Before the group can go on to the next stage there has to be a large measure of trust. Trusting leaves us open to breach of trust by others, to betrayal and to the risk of being hurt, but without a doubt, it is the most important development at this stage. If there are any feelings of mistrust among members there will be no energy to deal with tasks: all the energy will be used in defensive, protective action.

Until we have a solid basis of cooperation, a strong team spirit and a sense of unity, it will be difficult to go on to the next phase, that of completing the group task. But once all these things have been accomplished, the group energy can be directed to the task and work will flow.

5

CONSTRUCTION

HAVING REACHED THIS stage the group could, in theory, go on forever. But nothing lasts forever and there is actually just one more stage after this. For now, we'll look at the developments that happen during this constructive stage.

Group maintenance should be taking a lot less effort by now. Members should feel very comfortable with one another. There will still be disagreements, but those involved will be able to agree to disagree. The familiarity which has developed should enable everyone to be supportive and understanding even when they don't quite agree.

During this stage, which will be quite a long one for most groups, the main energy thrust will be directed toward getting the task or tasks completed. As the name 'construction' suggests, the real work of the group will be done during this stage.

Remember, though, that the move from one stage to another is not something that happens in a flash. Even though we can divide the process into five stages in our discussion, there is no clear line between them in real life. The growth from one stage to another will be slow and probably quite rough. There may be overlap when most of the members seem to have reached stage three and one or two members are still having the type of problems that crop up in stage two. Don't worry about it.

Perhaps the conflict can be resolved by having a member of the team act as an adviser or observer and helping the others to talk the problem through. If this doesn't work, you could try an independent counsellor, perhaps a friend if it's a family dispute or the personnel officer if it's a work team problem. As a last resort, the people in conflict may have to be asked to leave the group. You may find that one or both of the people having difficulty will leave the group of their own accord. This may solve the problem, and then again, it may not. If the person who remains is aggressive or disruptive they will seek a new contestant. The group may be losing some good talent because of one member's aggressive or disruptive behaviour.

Most of the other problems should have been sorted out by this stage and the team should have a good working relationship and a sound knowledge of one another's strengths and weaknesses.

INTERDEPENDENCE AND INDEPENDENCE

Independence is the ability to get on with things without too much pushing from anyone else. It encompasses self-reliance—the knowledge that you can trust your own judgement and opinions. In a group, this characteristic needs to be utilised for the good of the group. The member who can get things done quickly and reliably can be the greatest asset the group has, but if the independent person wants the glory for themselves they will cause a lot of friction.

The kind of independent behaviour we need in groups is the kind that sees what needs to be done and gets on with the job. It certainly isn't the kind we saw in chapter 4 when Wayne refused to become part of the group and kept operating as an independent individual. We can maintain our individuality and still pool our information, our resources and our efforts. In this way, the group will be strengthened and the result will be greater than the sum of the parts.

Interdependence, on the other hand, is the ability to rely on other members of the group to do the jobs allocated to them. We don't want to have to check up on one another all the time. It is important to the functioning of the group that all members should do their part, but also that they should feel confident that other members are doing theirs.

COMMITMENT

The dictionary definition of commitment is an obligation that restricts freedom of behaviour or movement. Once we join a group or team we take on the responsibility of behaving in a way which will be of benefit to the group as a whole. How we cope with this responsibility depends on our attitude toward and our behaviour within the group.

In the early stages of the group process, commitment may not be very strong. We are unsure of our role in the group, we don't know who the leader will be, we don't even know whether we are going to stay in the group or if the group will survive. Once these issues have been resolved and providing that we feel we have been an important part of making those decisions, we will feel that we have committed ourselves to the group. This helps to give us a sense of belonging, and once we feel that, we will be prepared to give up some of our personal freedom for the good of the team.

We need to realise, though, that this is more difficult for some than for others. People who have been brought up in a competitive atmosphere may find it very hard to adjust to the cooperative climate which is essential to a group.

WARMTH

In some circles, it's common to talk of giving 'warm fuzzies', the opposite of which are 'cold pricklies'. As the names suggest, 'warm fuzzies' are the things we do which make other people feel warm and comfortable. When we pay someone a compliment—and mean it— that's a warm fuzzy! On the other hand, when we pass a sarcastic or cutting remark, that's a cold prickly.

It isn't difficult to pay compliments. We don't have to overdo it. And don't say things that are not sincere. The rule that seems to work best is: if you can't say something good, don't say anything at all. Let's look at some examples.

Sophie had trouble with compliments. She didn't know how to give them and she didn't know what to do with them when she got them. It used to go something like this:

Jane: Thanks for typing up that report for me. You did a really great job.

Sophie: Oh, it was nothing. I just did it in my lunch hour.

The report was twenty-five pages and took much more than just Sophie's lunch hour. She could have accepted the compliment this way:

Sophie: That's alright. I enjoyed doing it and it was interesting to read, too.

If Sophie hadn't enjoyed doing it, but had done it because she felt she owed Jane a favour, she could have replied this way:

Sophie: That's alright. I felt I owed you one.

There wasn't any need to say more than that. Quite often we feel that we have to say more, give reasons or explanations. This isn't always the case.

What about giving compliments? They don't have to be any big deal either. You could just say something quite simple—provided you really mean it—like 'That was a good idea you had back there in the meeting about staggering the tea breaks'. If you leave it at that and don't wait for the other person to say anything, you'll feel good about it and so will they.

Don't feel that you have to put yourself down in order to make the other person feel good. Don't say things like 'You're so efficient you make me feel incompetent'. Why should you feel incompetent because someone else is efficient? You could just as easily say 'I admire your efficiency'. Perhaps you could add 'I'd like to be like that'. But don't make yourself feel or sound bad. It doesn't do anyone any good.

FREEDOM

By the time the group gets to the construction stage, freedom is another concept which comes into play. Each member will have gained the freedom which comes out of trust. Group members know each other's strengths and weaknesses by now and, within the bounds of this knowledge, are happy to give each other the freedom to do tasks their own way.

AGREEING TO DISAGREE

The group should now be working well together. Members will have reached a point where they can trust each other's judgement enough to be able to agree to disagree.

This means that each group member will be able to say, 'Yes, I see your point of view, but I feel differently about this matter. We won't be able to resolve the difference and it really won't matter if you keep believing this and I keep believing that. The main thing is for the task to progress.'

Many times when a group is working on a project, there will be disagreement over some small matters. In the earlier stages I said it was important to discuss any disagreements and resolve them before going on. In the process part of group communications this is important because it affects bonding, conflict resolution and negotiating skills. If there is going to be a team spirit and task orientation then it is important to ensure agreement. But once trust and team spirit have been established, there is room for disagreement without causing a rift. Members can respect one another's opinions without feeling threatened by a difference.

ADAPTABILITY

If you're adaptable, you're able to make changes to your ideas, your ideals and your behaviour. It can be something as simple as lowering your standards and letting the kids do the cooking when they can't make a wonderful baked dinner the way you do. They may not even make scrambled eggs as well as you do, but they have to learn and you have to give them the opportunity. And you have to eat the mess to give them positive, encouraging feedback.

In a group of adults you have to be adaptable or, like the tree that doesn't bend to the wind, you'll break. Behaviour patterns which are too rigid bring on nervous breakdowns and paranoia. People who are fanatical about anything are very difficult to work with. They believe that everyone should conform to their behaviour and their beliefs.

Peter, in our first case study, believed that women were not capable of taking on leadership roles. He also had a lot of other deepseated beliefs, which reinforced his feeling of superiority. He was not prepared to accept that things could change, so when they did he became aggressive and confrontational and in the end he was asked to leave the group.

SUPPORT

The more supportive our behaviour towards others, the less likely that they will try to read hidden meanings into the things we say. When the atmosphere in a group is not supportive, then everyone will be on the defensive, looking out for any sign of personal attack.

These are the characteristics of a supportive climate. There is:

- *Description* rather than evaluation of ideas put forward;
- *Problem orientation* rather than control;
- *Spontaneity* rather than strategy;
- *Empathy* rather than neutrality;
- *Equality* rather than superiority;
- *Open-mindedness* rather than certainty.

Let's look at them one by one. If the sender of a communication seems to be judging or evaluating the receiver in any way, then the receiver will become defensive. There are all sorts of factors involved here. For example, the words may be evaluative, but the tone of voice and the facial expression may show sincerity and openness. The listener is then less likely to become defensive. Remember, we pay a lot of attention, often without being aware that we are doing so, to the non-verbal behaviour of others. We are more likely to believe the signals we observe than the words we actually hear. In order to be supportive we have to take care not to make moral judgements— deciding what is good and bad—in a situation where this is not relevant.

Problem orientation means we are trying to work on a problem without trying to contol the other person. We concentrate on the problem rather than the behaviour of others in the group. The trouble with wanting to control others is that we are sending them a hidden message which says they are inadequate, or ignorant, or unable to make their own decisions and that we want to help them to change in some way. It is important to realise that most of the time our communications are directed at influencing someone. We are usually trying to get some other person to do something, or to change their attitude or to stop doing something they are doing. If we can change our own communication pattern from one of control to one of problem orientation, we will have come a long way towards improving the supportiveness in the group.

Spontaneity is the opposite of manipulation and deceit. When we feel we are being deceived or manipulated we become defensive. None of us likes to feel that we are being used as a pawn in someone else's game. The person who tries to use a strategy or a gimmick or who appears calculating usually causes others to behave in a defensive way. When our behaviour is genuinely spontaneous we are seen as being sincere, honest and non-threatening.

Empathy is the ability to feel what the other person is feeling and is one of the most supportive behaviours possible. It is the feeling of understanding which comes from a real sense of the worth of the other person. Some people talk of 'vibes' and when the vibes are good there is empathy. In contrast, if you're totally neutral you can appear to the other person to be disinterested or lacking in concern for their welfare. When you feel that the speaker is treating you just as a specimen to be studied, you resent them and their attitude. You wouldn't feel at all cooperative towards them.

High level support is dependent mainly on a combination of empathy and understanding, as well as all the other factors in this section.

Another way we cause people to feel defensive is by communicating to them, one way or another, that we consider ourselves superior to them in some way. Once we communicate these messages the other person feels inadequate or resentful, and this is not a supportive situation. What we need to signify is equality. Each of us is as good as the other. In a group, we need to work together on an equal footing.

Last on our list was open-mindedness, which is preferable to certainty. When we are totally sure of ourselves we become dogmatic. We are no longer open to suggestions from others. As soon as we give the impression that we know everything, people become defensive, put up a wall and refuse to listen. As long as we show that we are genuinely interested in solving problems we will get the help we need. Only when we seem to know all the answers do we cause people to become defensive.

Supportive behaviour, then, is made up of all these elements and we can all examine our own attitudes and behaviour in regard to these and decide whether we need to make any changes. Even quite small changes in attitude can make a big difference to our ability to communicate well.

SELF-CONFIDENCE

When we succeed we put it down to our own competence and effort, but when we fail we put it down to such factors as bad luck or the difficulty of the task. Now, this is all very well, but when we work in groups we need to beware of blaming other members for our failures. It is important not to boost our own self-confidence at the expense of other people in the group. It is too easy to ask cliched questions like 'How can I soar like an eagle when I'm surrounded by turkeys?' Are you sure you are an eagle? Self-confidence is admirable until it turns into a superiority complex. No one likes the person who is always right, always knows better and thinks they do no wrong.

DEVIATION

Deviating means behaving in a way which is not acceptable to other members of the group. The deviation may be as simple as a member not conforming to the way the rest of the group dresses or even styles their hair. Obviously, if the deviation is not too great there will be some tolerance, but it will probably be reluctant. On the other hand, if the deviation is severe, the group will deal with it.

There are four possible reasons why we would become deviates once we have become members of a group. First, we may have joined another group and become influenced by its norms. We bring the norms from the new group into our original group and find that they don't fit. We are rejected along with our deviations.

The second possibility is that we have personality characteristics which prevent us from accepting a norm. The group may be particularly interested in exploring as many possibilities as it can think of when making decisions. It goes on looking for different angles and solutions long after you would have made a decision. You try to speed up the decision-making process and annoy everyone.

Thirdly, you may have thought of something no one else has thought of. Because the idea is so wild, others don't want to consider it. This can also make you seem like a deviate.

Fourthly, deviation can occur as a means of challenging the leadership of the group. A member who would like to become leader may begin by disagreeing with everything the current leader says or does. At first this may be seen as deviation and could cause problems in the group.

Those are the reasons for deviation. Now let's look at how the group deals with deviates. At first there will be an increase in the amount of communication between the deviate and the rest of the group. Most of this will be started by other members of the group. They will be trying to persuade the deviate to change, to conform to the norms of the group. Perhaps some members may take the deviate aside and speak to him as a friend giving advice.

The problem at this early stage of deviance is that the group feels that its beliefs are being questioned. We all need to feel comfortable with our system of norms and beliefs, so we can react in one of two ways when it is questioned. The most common way of reacting is to become more rigid in our hold on what we believe. The other, much more difficult, reaction is to re-examine our beliefs. We will go through this re-examination process only when the deviate has a lot of power and influence, but even then we will feel threatened and vulnerable.

When the attempts at persuasion fail, and the increased level of communication is not having the desired effect, the next step is cessation of communication between the group and the deviate. The deviate will be excluded from activities, perhaps from meetings and, eventually, if they don't make any effort to conform, they will be expelled from the group.

This is drastic behaviour, but we see it around us every day. Most religions have procedures for expelling deviates from their communities. Other societies and organisations have rules written into their constitutions concerning how to deal with deviates. Of course, they don't all call them deviates.

Remember, groups have considerable power and influence over their members. After all, in a lot of cases we join groups because they satisfy some need we have, and the more we conform to the norms of the group, the better will those needs be satisfied.

Deviating from the norms of the group can produce varied results: it may make the norms more explicit and show clearly what happens to those who defy the norms, but it may also unleash new ideas. It is possible for deviant behaviour to appear at any stage of the group process, but it is more likely to be noticeable during the construction stage because it will be more disruptive. During the earlier stages of the group life, while bonds are still being formed, the team spirit is still being nurtured and leadership has not been finalised, the person who deviates too drastically will simply be expelled or rejected.

However, during the task-oriented construction stage, the deviate will be tolerated or not, according to whether or not he has high standing in the group. If the person has become a highly valued member, the deviation is more likely to influence and be accepted by other members.

EVALUATION

As a task proceeds it is important to evaluate progress and results. To do this we need to be clear about the goals we have. When these goals are well defined and explicit we have little or no trouble in seeing whether we are heading in the right direction or not.

We all practice evaluation even though we often do it subconsciously. It is a process of review, reflection and reassessment. It usually occurs at times when there are natural breaks in the action; something is completed and we have space and time to look at what has been done, what will be done next and what still needs to be done, always bearing in mind what the end goal is. This process is important and should be done more frequently than it usually is, because it helps keep the group or individual on track.

So, in a task situation evaluation is concerned with results. In a process assessment situation, or in a more personal sense, evaluation is a judgement of skills learned, situations experienced, new knowledge acquired and examination of growth which has taken place.

Self-evaluation—honestly done—can be a very good coping mechanism to get through stressful situations and new experiences. Make a list of all the skills you think are important for the situation under review. Wherever possible, break them down into the most specific skills. For example, don't just list 'running meetings', break this down to specific items such as 'setting agendas', 'booking venues', 'taking minutes'. Once you've set up a list check off—perhaps using different coloured pens—all items you knew before, all things you have learned well during the current activity and then things with which you have become familiar but don't feel able to do very well yet. This should cover everything on your list because anything you don't know about at all wouldn't have made it to the list in the first place.

Having done this, there are two steps you can take. The first, which is the one that relieves the stress, is to give yourself a pat on the back (or a treat) for the new skills you've learnt. The second is to go back through the skills in this book and see what, if anything, has been left off your list. These are skills you'll need to learn more about next time.

GROWING OLD

The only thing which will prevent the total disintegration of a group is constant change. This change will appear as growth though it won't actually be that. After all, growth implies an increase in size or strength or area of influence but we all know that it is not possible to go on growing forever. There is a German proverb that no tree ever grew right up to the sky.

For a moment we'll look at the changes which can prevent a group from dying. First, there's the regular flow of new members, bringing new ideas which the group accepts and adopts. Until members leave, this will constitute growth; once there is a drop in membership, new members will be replacing the shortfall so growth becomes maintenance of numbers. Religious sects and organisations like Rotary and Lions fit this description.

Another type of change occurs when a group is a good cohesive team which, as it completes one task, finds another goal to aim for. An example of this type of group is a large, possibly extended, family which stays together, taking care of one another's interests through several generations. The important aspect of the group's long life is its ability to change and adapt as time goes by.

Now, let's examine the behaviour and emotions of members of a group which is about to reach the last stage in our five-step plan of group development.

As it becomes obvious to members that the group's work, and therefore its life, is coming to an end, there will be a heightened sense of warmth toward other members of the group. People may feel a little confused, lethargic or frenzied, depending on the amount of work to be completed. There may be anger as people feel that they are no longer needed and resentment at being deprived of an enjoyable activity.

For those who did not altogether enjoy the experience of group work, there may be feelings of relief. But this may bring on a feeling, in some, of guilt at breaking off relationships with people with whom they felt they had little in common. Evaluation sessions may be painful for some; surprising for others; but for everyone they should be a time of constructive feedback.

Because stage four is usually the longest stage in the life of the group, we tend to overlook the fact that stage five will eventually take place. Just as we don't really want to face the fact that all who live must die, we also find it hard to accept that the group will also die. We try to hold on to the friendships which have formed, even romanticise them, making them out to be more important, warmer, friendlier than they really were. We talk about reunions, about meeting again, but don't really mean what we say.

These issues will be discussed in greater detail in the next chapter when we talk about 'crumbling'.

SUMMARY

Although this stage is the longest in the life of the group, it's concerned mainly with tasks. Most of what happens in the process of the group in this stage is maintenance behaviour.

On the whole, by this stage in the life of the group, members should feel warm and comfortable with one another. The atmosphere in the group should be supportive and there should be interdependence as well as independence. The commitment to the group task should be high and so should the level of trust between members.

Everyone should have a good self-image. Self-esteem, brought about by encouragement from one another and the achievement of goals, should also be high. By this stage there should be little dissension within the group, and there may even be some social interaction, but this need not be the case. When the group has worked together for a considerable amount of time close bonds may have formed, and these will make disintegration difficult. It will be painful for some members to accept that the group will no longer exist.

Deviation, which we discussed earlier in this chapter, can occur at other times in the life of the group, but it is only in this stage, when so much of the team spirit has already been established that it can cause a lot of problems. In earlier stages, the deviate would be kept in check, or rejected completely and expelled from the group quite quickly. During the construction stage, when there is a higher level of commitment to the group and to the task, and people trust each other, the deviate will have to be dealt with in a manner that will be satisfactory for everyone—those who like and trust the deviate as well as those who don't.

Not much can go wrong in the construction stage, but if something does go awry it helps to use this as a learning experience. The group should have built up enough trust to be able to assess and evaluate any problems which arise without hurting anyone's feelings. The social–emotional leader should be able to resolve any misunderstandings tactfully and the task leader should have, or have acquired, the skill to solve any practical problems that may arise. Much of what caused difficulty or irritations in the earlier stages should be resolved by now and problems which arise during this stage are usually isolated and limited in scope.

6

CRUMBLING

A GROUP, AS you will have realised by now, is a living thing, and like all living things, it will eventually die. This may sound harsh, but if we face up to this it will be a little less traumatic. There are ways in which we can prepare ourselves for this stage and the possible void after it.

Even when we don't consciously think about it, there are behaviour patterns we learnt in other situations which will be useful here. Along the way we have had to part company with other people and groups we have known. When you went from one school to another, even if it was only from primary to high school, your group changed to a greater or lesser extent. You lost touch with people. You may have been really good friends while you saw each other every day, but once you were put in separate schools or even just separate classes you drifted apart.

That is one form of disengagement. For some it is a painful process, for others it is hardly noticeable. How we feel about this process depends to a large extent on what we do to fill the gap. For the person who leads a busy life, other things soon take up the time and other people become more important.

For those who don't have other people and places there can be severe confusion, conflict and anger. But at the same time there will be a warmth which may not have been there earlier. Most of us have a tendency to look at our memories through rose-coloured glasses: we remember the good rather than the bad from our past experiences. And so it will be when we look back, during this crumbling stage, on the work of the group. If we were part of the success of the group, we will have a warm rosy glow about the group and all the members. On the other hand, if we felt that our contribution was not successful, or something we spent a lot of time on was not used, we may feel lethargic or angry. We may go into a frenzy of activity in an attempt to improve our self-image, to prove—at least to ourselves—that we are capable and useful.

During this stage the group will look more and more to the person who has been the social–emotional leader for help in coping with the emotions which surface.

When this stage draws to a close, you should assess what you have achieved and what you have gained from the experience. Naturally, you will first list things related to the group task or tasks. You may decide that you learnt a lot about the dangers of asbestos, or how to win a football match. You may even realise that you learnt how to run a meeting.

You also learnt a lot of personal skills, such as listening, negotiating, dealing with conflict and a whole lot more. All these, which can be called portable skills, are areas of expertise which you take with you to your next job, your next group or team, to your personal relationships and to your family for the rest of your life. It's amazing how we grow through even seemingly unrelated events in our lives.

SOCIAL–EMOTIONAL EMPHASIS

The crumbling stage is when the person with social–emotional leadership qualities really comes into their own. They will be the one everybody else turns to as the painful process of group disintegration begins. Dealing with grief is different for each of us, but the person with empathy will be able to deal with the whole range of behaviour exhibited by other group members.

It is important that this stage be dealt with in a caring and sharing way. Leaving people to deal with difficult emotions on their own, especially if they haven't had to do it before, can be destructive. Probably the most important thing the leader can do is to listen sympathetically. Just talking things through is usually a great help.

CONFUSION

Confusion comes about during this time because we begin to feel dislocated from our normal activities. Meetings of the group may become fewer and further apart. We begin to experience a sense of loss and because we may not recognise it we feel confused. Suddenly we may find that we need to make contact with other members, even though there is nothing to talk about. We call them on the phone, or pop in to their offices and then wonder why. They may do the same, and we both feel embarrassed. This is usually when members begin to realise that the group is about to disintegrate.

Any small details of task which need completion may pose difficulties which would have seemed insignificant at other stages. Now, because of a general feeling of dissatisfaction and confusion, they may seem insurmountable. This may be an attempt to keep the group together a little longer. It may be that the feelings of confusion and anger beginning to surface will actually make the work more difficult.

CONFLICT

In the early part of this stage there may be increased conflict between group members. This is even more likely if the group is a family. As the time draws close for the group to break up, for the family to part, for grown children to leave home, there will be arguments and discussions which become heated to the point of causing hurt and anger.

Some psychologists see this as a defence mechanism: we won't be hurt when we leave someone with whom we have had a fight. When we think about it rationally, we realise that this is not really a good way to part; it makes it more difficult to get back together at a later stage. Reconciliations become more difficult as time goes by. Counsellors and therapists feel that it is better to resolve conflicts before the final parting of the ways so that no one bears a grudge or carries an emotional burden around with them for ages afterwards.

ANGER

Although we may feel angry about the break, we don't usually show it in a recognisable form. Something like kicking the cat is what actually happens: we take it out in other ways. Perhaps you are angry about your family breaking up but you don't want to upset the other members of the household who all seem to be accepting the situation. At home you behave in a normal, cheerful way as though nothing is wrong. In the office, during the day, all you can think of is how the breakup is going to affect your life: how lonely you will be without your adult child. Your work suffers. You snap at people you work with and they don't understand why, at least until you confide in someone and they pass the message round. This behaviour is called displacement: we transfer our feeling of anger away from the cause to other areas of our lives. For those around us this can be confusing and disturbing and needs explanation. Hopefully it will bring us a little sympathy, but I wouldn't really wait for this. We need to deal with our feelings ourselves.

Another way of dealing with this kind of anger is called sublimation. In this case we transfer the feelings of anger into doing things which are more socially valued. For example, we may decide to do some voluntary work with underprivileged people. One person I know paints her house when she is angry, another digs up his garden. These activities get rid of the energy generated by the anger while still being socially acceptable. You may find that any physical activity which gives you time to think things through will help to get the anger under control.

WARMTH

Towards the end of the group's existence there is likely to be a sudden surge of warmth between members who, until now, have not shown each other much affection. It is almost as if we want to leave people with good feelings and memories of us. It's interesting to note that this behaviour is seldom misunderstood: we intuitively realise what is happening because we also want to be remembered as warm, friendly people.

We accept the offers and return the feelings and it's possible that we do this only because we are aware of the coming parting. This is not to say that our feelings are not genuine: they are, but they are tolerated and returned only because we know that the involvement will not be long-term. Many of us are afraid to become too involved with other people. We are happy to keep most of our relationships on a superficial level and not get emotionally involved for fear that in the end someone will be hurt. In a group which is soon to cease existence, it is easier to show feelings which we know will be temporary.

RECOGNITION OF END

For some it may be difficult to see the end, and this is where the social–emotional leader of the group will show their strength. This leader, (and remember he or she may not be the actual group leader) will be able to help any member who is having trouble accepting the demise of the group. It will take a fair bit of talking and a lot of listening to help get people through the grief and anger they may feel.

The best way, from my experience, of dealing with grief is to start planning future goals before the end is actually reached. Sometime during stage four, when the work on the task is well underway, start looking around for a new group or a new project, either for yourself or, if others agree, for the group as a whole. You don't have to start working on it yet, but just knowing that there is something to look forward to is a great help in dealing with the grieving which is inevitable.

LETHARGY

Sometime during the transition from stage four to stage five it will seem as if some or maybe even all the members of the group have run out of steam. This is one of the surest signs that stage five is

90

about to begin. During stage four, energy levels should be fairly high all the time. Of course, individual members may have bad patches: somebody may be ill, or distracted by outside responsibilities or just plain tired. But the group as a whole should have developed some momentum and the task should progress well.

As the end of the task comes into view, there will probably be some slowing down. There are two reasons for this: one is that there is not so much to be done (provided there is no deadline pressure); the other is a natural desire to prolong the process because of the reluctance to break up the group.

FRENZY

This is the opposite of lethargy and occurs when the group has a deadline to meet in the completion of the task. It may be a presentation to the company management; in a family it may be a wedding or a departure date for a long separation; in a study group it could be an upcoming exam. If the work is incomplete and the deadline is looming, there will be frenzied activity which will cause a whole series of problems.

Conflict will increase in frequency and intensity. Emotions will be running high: people will be easily upset, egos will be fragile. This, again, will be a time for the leadership of the social–emotional person in the group. But it will also be a test of the task leader. The first is needed to pour oil on troubled waters and the second to ensure that everything gets done.

By the time the end is reached there will either be feelings of tremendous relief and then friendship if things went well, or the stress will have reached explosion point and everyone will be happy it's all over. In this latter case, stage five may actually be a relief and there will be no sad parting. Everyone will just be glad it's all over and done.

EVALUATION OF PERSONAL SKILLS AND KNOWLEDGE OF GROUP PROCESS

By the time you have been in a group long enough to get to stage five, it is definitely worthwhile taking stock of what you have learnt. That's something this book can help you with. By going back over all the sub-headings and the case studies, you can make an inventory of what you have learnt. Any topic you feel you didn't learn enough about during your time with the group, you can read through carefully and think about. This is also a learning process.

Once you have completed your group task, you should remember to add this information to your resumé. It will stand you in good stead when next you apply for a promotion or a new job. You should also add all the new skills you acquired in the course of working on the task. You probably learned something about the subject which may have been new to you. You may also have acquired skills like note-taking, report writing, gathering information and finding resources. All these skills are portable: you take them with you to your next group, your next task, your next job.

DISENGAGEMENT

This is the process which flows from stage four through to the end of stage five. It is, for most of us, a difficult process. The longer we have been involved with a group, the more difficult it becomes to separate ourselves from it. This reluctance to disengage ourselves can take several forms.

As we've already seen, we may try to increase the frequency of contact with other members, hoping that this will make up for the fact that we know the group is coming to an end. We also know that some of us get angry and resentful, and seem almost to be seeking conflict and bad feelings. This is one way of trying to justify the imminent demise of the group. The thinking behind this seems to be that if we fight with the rest of the group we will be right in leaving and it won't hurt so much. Then there are the people who try to fade out. When the task is nearing completion they start missing meetings, come late, don't answer messages, and just generally seem to be avoiding the group. This is just another coping mechanism, and we need to be understanding when we come up against this kind of behaviour.

Another phenomenon you may have experienced, perhaps when

a large family or a school leaving class was breaking up, is the talk about reunions. Groups of people who retire after working in the same company for many years also promise to meet again in one or three or whatever number of years. Mostly these meetings just don't happen. When they do they will be so stilted and uncomfortable for almost everyone who turns up that each year there will be fewer who attend. If you've ever been to a school reunion you'll understand. Unless you were one of the lucky ones who never upset anyone in any way—I know a woman like this who always enjoys reunions— these meetings usually become a contest in one-upmanship.

INDIVIDUALITY AND SEPARATENESS

Maintaining your individuality and separateness from the group is important. If the group becomes your total existence then the end of the group will be all the more traumatic. Building a new life afterwards will be more difficult, take longer and leave you with very little self-esteem or self-worth. It is important to remain self-reliant and have a separate existence, a separate life. When the life of the group becomes your whole life, beware. This can happen in religious groups, friendship groups, workplace groups and families.

When groups exert so much influence over members that grown people cannot make any decisions, however small, without consulting the group, that's dangerous. Usually this kind of situation is the result of very strong leadership: one person has more control than is normal and other members of the group become totally dependent. If the group is a religious sect, strange things can happen. A well-known example is the Jonestown mass suicides. Everyone there was so dependent on the leader that when he said 'die', everyone did.

Keeping your individuality in the face of this type of leadership can be difficult. After all, we all like to take the line of least resistance. It is so easy to let others make decisions for us, so effortless to just go along with the group. But if we don't keep making our own decisions and living our own lives, then when the leader folds up his tent and goes home alone, we are left powerless and unable to make any decisions through lack of practice.

The more you practise making decisions and then living with them, the better you become at it. So, don't be afraid. If you haven't had much practice at it, start now. Make small decisions, like what to wear today, and very soon you'll be making bigger ones, like setting off on a voyage of discovery and you won't regret it.

CONCLUSION

In the limited space which a book allows us, we have examined the processes in the life of a group. For those of you who would like to evaluate the groups you belong to now, or will join in the future, the checklist which follows should be helpful. Once you have responded to the statements it should be a simple matter of checking your answers in the column headed 'Mostly No' and referring to the relevant topics in the previous sections of this book. With a little thought and some tactful intervention you will find that it is usually not too difficult to overcome most problems. Of course, this isn't always the case. As I have said in several other places, sometimes, for the good of the group as a whole, it may be necessary to ask somebody to leave. This is a painful process for all concerned—the person being asked to leave, the person doing the asking and everyone else in the group as well, and should be done as gently and tactfully as possible.

CHECKLIST

CHECK YOUR GROUP'S effectiveness. By putting a tick in either the 'Mostly Yes' or 'Mostly No' column you will be able to identify areas of difficulty at a glance.

	Mostly Yes	Mostly No
1 The atmostphere is relaxed and comfortable.		
2 People listen to each other's suggestions and ideas.		
3 There is a well-established, relaxed working relationship among the members.		
4 Group members understand what they are trying to accomplish.		
5 Group discussion is frequent and it is usually pertinent to the task.		
6 There is a cooperative, rather than a competitive, relationship among group members.		
7 There is general agreement on most courses of action.		
8 Disagreements are tolerated and an attempt is made to resolve them.		
9 Suggestions and criticisms are offered and received in a helpful spirit.		
10 The group welcomes frank criticism from inside and outside sources.		

	Mostly Yes	Mostly No

11 There is a high degree of trust and confidence between the leader and other members.

12 The leader and members hold a high opinion of the group's capabilities.

13 The group members strive hard to help the group achieve its goal.

14 When the group takes action, clear assignments are given and accepted.

15 The leader of the group is well suited to the job.

16 There is ample communication within the group about topics relevant to getting the work accomplished.

17 People are kept busy but not overloaded.

18 The group goals are set high but not so high as to create anxieties or fear of failure.

19 Creativity is stimulated within the group.

20 Group members feel confident in making decisions.

It's possible that the items you have ticked under the 'Mostly No' heading look like rather a long list. Don't try to fix everything at once. Rather, look up the topics which occur early in the book and work on them first. Fix one or two items at a time. Any more than that will cause confusion and disorientation. For instance, if you found that your group does not stick to the point very well when discussing the group task (checkpoint 5), you could steer conversation back to the group topic when it strays. If it keeps happening you could point out the problem, and get the others in the group to help overcome it.

Like all other skills we learn, working with groups takes practice. Just keep trying and take every opportunity you can to join a group whose goals interest you. You'll soon get the hang of it.

INDEX

Note: Similar words have been listed under one entry, e.g. 'accept', 'acceptance', 'accepted', etc. are all listed under 'acceptance'.

acceptance, xiii, 28, 47, 51, 52, 59
adaptability, 77
affection, xiv, 17, 20, 51, 52, 54, 62, 66
agenda, 21, 31, 32; secret agenda, 38
agree to disagree, 77
agreement, xii, 42, 55, 73
aggressive, 13, 15, 74
angry, 89
anxiety, 18, 28
approval, 14, 39
assertiveness, xii, 13–16, 18, 47, 59; non-assertive, 13–15
attitude, 10, 59, 62
authority, xiii, 46, 47

behaviour, xiv, 10, 26, 30, 34, 35, 37, 38, 59, 60, 62, 77, 79
beliefs, 10, 59, 61, 62, 64, 81
belonging, xiii, 10
bigotry, 17
body language, 1, 7, 8, 18
boredom, 17, 18
brainstorming, 53, 54

change, 2, 21, 60, 62, 68, 77, 79, 83, 84
clarifier, 38
commitment, xii, 29, 37, 75, 85
compromise, 42
confidence, 11, 20, 40
conflict, xiv, 27, 30, 42, 43, 74, 86, 87, 88, 91
conflict resolution, xi, 19, 42

conformity, 68, 69
confusion, 86, 88
cooperative, 30, 38, 40, 55, 62, 67, 71, 72
creativity, x
criticism, xiv, 30
culture, 9, 10

decision making, xii, 53, 54, 56, 93, 94
delegating, 70–1
deviate, xiv, 80–2, 85
disagreement, 47, 73, 77
discussion, 16, 54
disengagement, 86, 92
disintegrate, xiii, 11, 83
displacement, 89
disruptive, 74
dress, 9, 59

effectiveness, 70
emotion, xi, 17, 18
empathy, 49, 79, 87
equality, 79
evaluation, 33, 82, 84
expel, 9

family group, ix, x, xii, 2, 11, 43, 56, 87, 91, 93
feedback, 2, 7, 65, 71
feelings, 17, 26; hurt feelings, 14, 18
freedom, xii, 76
frenzy, 91
friction, 62

gestures, 7–9
give and take, 58
goal, 11, 16, 26, 27, 40, 44, 82, 84; achievable, 44
grievance, 13

group building, 39
group maintenance, 39, 73, 85
groupthink, 69
growth, xv, 29

humility, 39, 49

ignored, 9
I-language, 15
incentive, 44
inclusion, xiii
independence, 2, 74, 85
individuality, 67, 93
influence, xiv, 2, 12
inhibitions, 52
initiative, 60
interdependence, xiv, 74, 85
interpersonal communication, xi
intimidated, 27
irritation, 17

judgement, 4, 28, 78

leader, formal and informal, 19, 20
leadership, 19, 26, 27, 36; struggles, xii, 24; temporary, 27
lethargy, 90
listening, 3–7, 28, 49, 51, 64, 65, 66, 90
loyalty, 52

manipulation, 79
meeting procedures, 20, 32; planning, 20
messages, self-defeating, 16; positive, 16
multiskilling, 12

negotiate, 42–4, 56–9, 77, 87
norms, 59, 80, 81, 82

observant, 28
open-minded, xiv, 51, 64, 79
opinions, 13, 29

participate, xiv, 12
people person, xv, 18, 19, 67
perception, 18, 19
personal skills, 87, 91
polite, 13, 14, 17, 29, 39
power, xiii, xiv, 30; struggles, xii, xiv, 30
prejudice, 17, 64
problem solving, 53
punish, 52, 53

questions, xi, 35, 36, 38

recognition, 90
reconciliation, 88
rejection, xiii, xiv
relaxation, 41
resentment, 84
resistance, passive, 37
respect, 14, 34, 40
ridiculed, 9, 18, 28
rights, 14, 15
risk taking, xi, 28, 29, 39, 49
risky shift, 69, 70
roles, 26, 37, 38
rules, 34, 35

sabotage and subversion, 49, 50
self-concept, 10
self-confidence, 80

self-esteem, 16, 17, 40, 85
self-evaluation, 83
self-image, 85
separateness, 93
signs and signals, 8, 9, 18
social-emotional leader, xv, 19, 20, 85, 87, 90, 91
speaking, xi, 1, 4, 5, 6, 14, 65
spokesperson, 20
spontaneity, 79
status, 36
stress management, 41, 42
subversion, 42
success, 16, 17
support, xiv, 38, 78, 79, 80

task leader, 19, 20, 85, 91
tolerance, 17, 26, 80; intolerance, 17
transition, 29
trust, xii, xiv, xv, 11, 20, 39, 40, 49, 51–4, 66, 67, 85; builder, 67

undermine, 37, 45

values, 62
verbal communication, 1, 3; non-verbal communication, 1, 7, 78
viewpoint, 19

warmth, 75, 89
win-win, 42, 51, 58, 59